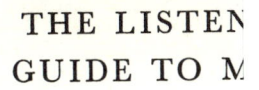

THE LISTEN[ER'S]
GUIDE TO M[USIC]

THE FULL ORCHESTRA

THE LISTENER'S GUIDE TO MUSIC

With a Concert-goer's Glossary

BY

PERCY A. SCHOLES

TENTH EDITION

OXFORD UNIVERSITY PRESS

Oxford University Press, Walton Street, Oxford OX2 6DP

OXFORD LONDON GLASGOW
NEW YORK TORONTO MELBOURNE WELLINGTON
KUALA LUMPUR SINGAPORE JAKARTA HONG KONG TOKYO
DELHI BOMBAY CALCUTTA MADRAS KARACHI
IBADAN NAIROBI DAR ES SALAAM CAPE TOWN

ISBN 0 19 284002 9

Tenth Edition, 1942
First published by Oxford University Press, London, 1919

*First issued as an Oxford University Press paperback, 1961
and reprinted in 1962, 1965, 1968, 1972, 1974, and 1978*

All rights reserved. No part of this publication may be reproduced, stored in a retrieval system, or transmitted, in any form or by any means, electronic, mechanical, photocopying, recording, or otherwise, without the prior permission of Oxford University Press

This book is sold subject to the condition that it shall not, by way of trade or otherwise, be lent, re-sold, hired out, or otherwise circulated without the publisher's prior consent in any form of binding or cover other than that in which it is published and without a similar condition including this condition being imposed on the subsequent purchaser

*Printed in Great Britain
at the University Press, Oxford
by Vivian Ridler
Printer to the University*

TO THE CONCERT-GOER,
GRAMOPHONIST, AND RADIO LISTENER
ON BOTH SIDES OF THE ATLANTIC

CONTENTS

I.	SOME SIMPLE NECESSARY TERMS EXPLAINED	1
II.	WHAT THE LISTENER REALLY NEEDS TO KNOW	8
III.	HOW THE COMPOSER WORKS	11
IV.	ON THE PRINCIPLE OF DESIGN IN MUSIC	19
V.	HOW SMALL INSTRUMENTAL PIECES ARE MADE	24
VI.	ON THE MYSTERIES OF 'SONATA-FORM'	29
VII.	ON THE SONATA OR SYMPHONY AS A WHOLE	35
VIII.	'WHAT DO YOU MEAN BY YOUR MOUNTAINOUS FUGUES?'	42
IX.	ON 'PROGRAMME MUSIC'	48
X.	ON THE SONG, ON ORATORIO, AND ON OPERA	55
XI.	THE ORCHESTRA AND ITS INSTRUMENTS	57
XII.	SOME TYPICAL ORCHESTRAL COMBINATIONS	64
XIII.	THE CHAIN OF COMPOSERS	68
	APPENDIX: Books for Additional Reading	80
	CONCERT-GOER'S GLOSSARY	81

LIST OF PLATES

	The full orchestra	*Frontispiece*
		facing page
I.	The first violins	22
II.	Cellos and double-basses	22
III.	Piccolo and two flutes	23
IV.	French horns	23
V.	Bass clarinet, clarinets, and bassoons	54
VI.	Three trumpets	54
VII.	Three trombones and a tuba	55
VIII.	Timpani and percussion	55
	Score of an Elgar Symphony	*pages 70 and 71*

The photographs are reproduced by courtesy of the British Broadcasting Corporation, and the orchestral score of Elgar's Second Symphony by permission of Messrs. Novello & Co. Ltd.

ACKNOWLEDGEMENTS
(1919)

The Author gratefully acknowledges his obligations:

To Rev. Basil Yeaxlee, Ph.D., O.B.E., late Secretary of the Universities Committee of the British National Council of Y.M.C.A.'s, who encouraged him to prepare this book for the use of the soldier classes in *A Listener's Course in Music* in France, and elsewhere, towards the end of the 1914 war, and to the late Sir John D. McClure, Mus.D., LL.D., Chairman of the Music Committee of that Council, who added his approval and support.

To Mr. O. Kling, of Messrs. Chester & Co., for the loan of a set of over 300 Queen's Hall Promenade Concert Programmes used in the preparation of the Concert-goer's Glossary. To Mr. John Lane, for permission to use a lengthy quotation from d'Indy's *César Franck*. To Mr. Myles Birket Foster, F.R.A.M., whose *History of the Royal Philharmonic Society* has proved of service. To Dr. Arthur Somervell and Mr. Theodore Walrond, of the Board of Education, and to a number of readers in all parts of the world who have made suggestions as to small additions and alterations, many of which have been incorporated in successive editions.

To his former colleague, Mr. A. Forbes Milne, M.A., Mus.B., for his valuable advice and for help with the proofs.

SEVENTH EDITION

This has been carefully revised throughout, and the Author acknowledges the help in the process of Mr. C. M. Crabtree, B.A., Mus.B. As an instance of the strange way in which errors escape detection, it may be mentioned that six large editions of this book have been sold without anyone pointing out that the Author had described 'God save the King' as having *five* lines, or that the Opus number that belongs to the 'Waldstein' Sonata had been attached to the 'Eroica' Symphony.

EIGHTH, NINTH, AND TENTH EDITIONS

A few necessary small changes have been made, in each impression, to bring the book up to date.

CHAPTER I

SOME SIMPLE NECESSARY TERMS EXPLAINED

Before Music can be discussed in any detail certain ground must be cleared. If this book is to serve its full purpose the assumption must throughout be made that some of its readers 'do not know a thing about' music. The very names of the notes may be strange to them, the conception of 'key' may be novel, the rhythmic combinations implied in 'time-signatures' may have no meaning. And it is impossible to explain musical form without the use of the names of notes, the names of keys, and the names of 'times'. A chapter in which this and similar apparatus may be put at the reader's disposition must therefore follow. It may be dry, but it is necessary—and it is as short as possible.

NOTES

The sounds of nature range from 'low' to 'high' (to use purely conventional terms), proceeding by a mere smooth incline (to follow out the idea of those conventional terms). When a dog howls, a cat mews, or a cow moos, it is merely using a section of that incline, beginning at the lowest point of which its vocal chords are capable and proceeding to the highest, or vice versa. Birds do not glide like cats, they hop: their song, too, as it happens, proceeds not by a smooth movement but from point to point in the 'incline' of sounds. In other words, birds use notes—and so do humans, birds and humans being the only two truly musical families of the world's creatures.

SCALES AND KEYS

A bird inherits a little combination of notes from its ancestors and contents itself with repeating this over and over again as long as it lives. Man invents new combinations in infinite variety, consequently man needs a working system. He fixes on a certain series of notes with a definite relation to each other and makes his tunes out of these. Such a series is called a Scale. A Scale is simply the regiment of the notes used in a human tune, drawn up on parade, and made to number off.

It is found, as an acoustical fact, that any given note recurs at higher and lower pitches (of which the upper is said to be an octave above the lower—see footnote 2), so that the whole long staircase of notes is divided into a number of short flights of stairs, and these become the scale-units of music.

In normal European and American music each of these scale-units is divided into twelve equal parts,[1] of which seven[2] are chosen for chief service, the others being called on as auxiliaries. These seven may be chosen out of the twelve according to two systems. The one system produces what we call the Major Scale, the other the Minor Scale.

The twelve notes are divided from each other by intervals called 'semitones': two semitones make a tone. On the piano keyboard any two adjacent notes are a semitone apart; any two notes next-but-one to each other are a tone apart (whether white or black has nothing to do with it; there is no social distinction of colour—all enjoy equal rights of citizenship).

The Major Scale can be begun from any of the twelve notes by proceeding upwards as follows (1 = tone; ½ = semitone):

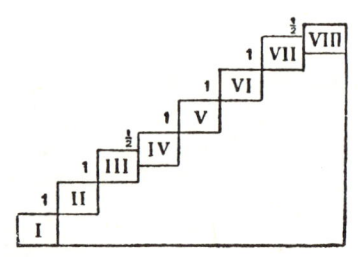

[1] Many of the statements in this book are practical rather than scientifically exact.

[2] Eight, instead of seven, if the main note be included both at top and bottom—hence the term Octave.

SOME SIMPLE NECESSARY TERMS EXPLAINED

The Minor Scale can be begun by proceeding upwards as follows:

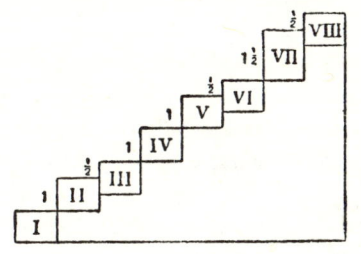

```
                              ½ ┌────┐
                           ┌───┤ VIII│
                        1½ │VII│    │
                     ½ ┌───┤   │    │
                    ┌──┤VI │   │    │
                  1 │V │   │   │    │
               ┌───┤  │   │   │    │
             1 │IV │  │   │   │    │
          ½ ┌──┤   │  │   │   │    │
         ┌──┤III│   │  │   │   │    │
       1 │II│   │   │  │   │   │    │
    ┌────┤  │   │   │  │   │   │    │
    │ I  │  │   │   │  │   │   │    │
```

[The arrangement of the notes VI and VII is sometimes varied slightly.]

The essential difference between the Major and Minor Scales is that in the lower part of the Major Scale the semi-tone occurs between III and IV, and in the lower part of the minor scale between II and III. Play a few scales Major and Minor, beginning on any note of the pianoforte and proceeding according to the diagrams just given, and the great difference of effect will be realized.

For convenience letter-names are given to the white notes of the piano as follows: A, B, C, D, E, F, G. The note next above any of these white notes is called its sharp, the one next below, its flat. A glance at the piano will show that on the keyboard sharps and flats generally fall on black notes, but that in two or three cases they fall on white notes, which white notes have thus not only their own proper names but also an additional name acquired from another note. (This is simple enough: you may speak of a man as Tom Brown, or you may speak of him as Bill Jones's neighbour.)

The object of our explanation so far has been to enable a reader who did not know a fact about our tonal system when he began this chapter to understand in future what is meant by such terms as 'C major' or 'D minor', 'G sharp minor' or 'B flat major'. A piece 'in' the key of C major is one of which the main prevailing choice of notes is made by the use of those found in the major scale beginning on the note C, and so forth. (Where the note C is found on the piano does not matter to the reader, but if he does not know the names of the notes on the piano and wants to do so he can get a friend to show him in two minutes, or he can make his own calculations from the starting-point of the first note on the left of the piano keyboard, which is A.)

MODULATION

Hardly any piece, however tiny, stays in one key. Even an Anglican chant to which the psalms are sung in church, with its mere ten notes, generally moves to another key about half-way through—that is to say, some flat or sharp is introduced in place of one of the original notes, and thus the key is altered. Such an alteration we call a Modulation.

A modulation, or a series of modulations is, however extended, merely an incident; the piece returns before its end to the key in which it started—which is felt to be *the* key of the piece.

A piece may modulate from any key to any key, but there are certain close relationships of key within which it is easier and apparently more natural to modulate. Thus we speak of 'Related Keys', and in a quite short piece it is likely that all modulations which occur will be to keys closely related to the main key of the piece.

RHYTHM AND TIME

The whole universe moves in rhythm, suns revolve and seasons change, tides rise and fall, flowers appear and die, hearts beat and horses trot according to a periodic system which we call by that name. Poems are written and declaimed (or ought to be declaimed) in rhythms. Regular beats or pulses and recurring accents can be felt in a line of poetry, and these occur also in music. These accents divide the line of poetry or phrase of music into rhythmic units. In both poetry and music there are felt to be either two beats or three beats, as the case may be, to each unit. If a phrase of music seems to have four beats to a unit these will be found to be really two units of two beats each, making together the larger group of four. Similarly, six beats fall into two sets of three, or three sets of two, and twelve beats into four sets of three.

The reader is now in a position to understand the 'Time-signatures' he sometimes sees quoted in concert programmes. The

SOME SIMPLE NECESSARY TERMS EXPLAINED

indication of $\frac{3}{4}$ means that there are three beats to a unit, or bar (neglect always the lower figure, which has no real significance except for the performer), $\frac{2}{2}$ has two beats, $\frac{6}{8}$ has two sets of three beats, and so forth.

Within each unit (or bar[1]) there may be, and generally are, smaller combinations—groups of half-beat notes or quarter-beat notes, two-beat notes, three-beat notes, one-and-a-half-beat notes, &c. There is thus possible an infinite variety of long and short notes and combinations of such, but underlying these shifting note-rhythms the regular rhythmic pulsation of the beats and bars can be felt.

Another part of the rhythmic system of Music is the use of 'Phrases' or 'Sentences'. In addition to its shifting rhythms of short notes and long ones, and its regular rhythms of beats and bars, any tune you may hear will be found to fall into equal or fairly equal lengths of (say) two or four bars apiece. Thus *God save the Queen*[2] has the time-signature of $\frac{3}{2}$ or $\frac{3}{4}$, i.e. its bar-rhythm consists of groups of three beats each. But its bars also fall into groups as follows:

3 Phrases making one Sentence:
- God save our gracious Queen (2 bars)
- Long live our noble Queen, (2 bars)
- God save the Queen: (2 bars)

4 Phrases making another Sentence:
- Send her victorious, (2 bars)
- Happy and glorious, (2 bars)
- Long to reign over us; (2 bars)
- God save the Queen. (2 bars)

The reader is now in a position to understand the words 'Beat', 'Bar', 'Phrase', and 'Sentence' when he meets them in annotated concert programmes.

[1] English *Bar* = American *Measure*.
[2] American readers know this tune as *My Country, 'tis of Thee*.

SOME SIMPLE NECESSARY TERMS EXPLAINED

MELODY, HARMONY AND COUNTERPOINT

The poet and the plain man often use the words 'Melody' and 'Harmony' interchangeably. By either they mean merely pleasant sound.

Technically used, as in a concert programme, the words have distinct meanings, Melody being a simple string of notes such as you could whistle or sing by yourself, and Harmony a combination of notes such as you could play with your hands on the piano. A handful of notes, whether sung by a choir or played by instruments, is called a 'Chord'. When you sing *God save the Queen* you are uttering Melody; if you sit down and accompany yourself by 'Chords' on the piano you are also producing 'Harmony'. Despite the poets, neither 'Melody' nor 'Harmony' necessarily connotes anything pleasant, in fact poor Melody and bad Harmony are very common. Moreover, new styles of Melody and Harmony are constantly being introduced to which many people object very much until they get used to them.

'Counterpoint' is simply a combination of melodies. A composer might take *God save the Queen*, leaving the existing tune for you to sing as before, but fit with it two or three other tuneful parts for two or three other voices to sing at the same time. You would then be singing your old 'Melody' and each of the other voices would have its Melody, the whole would be a piece of 'Counterpoint', and, further, since the voices sounding together would produce a series of 'Chords', there would be 'Harmony'.

It may be well to call attention to the adjective from 'Counterpoint', frequently used in later pages. It is 'Contrapuntal'. *God save the Queen* as sung by one person is 'Melodic'; as usually sung by a choir, or accompanied at the piano, it is *also* 'Harmonic'; as just arranged in imagination in the last paragraph it is, *further*, 'Contrapuntal'.

FORM

The relation of portions of a musical composition to each other and to the whole—fully explained in later chapters.

OPUS
(i.e. Latin for 'work')

This word will be found occasionally in the following pages, and frequently in concert programmes (often reduced to 'Op.'). Modern composers of the serious sort generally number their works as they produce them 'Op. 1' 'Op. 2', &c. Frequently several pieces are brought into one opus, and they are then numbered Op. I, No. 1; Op. 1, No. 2, &c. It is always worth while to notice an opus number, as it gives an idea as to whether a work represents its composer's early tentative stages or his maturity. In hearing an Op. 5, for instance, you must generally be a little indulgent. On the other hand, an Op. 50 or Op. 100 has no claim on your charity, and must be content to bear your fiercest criticism. This is generally true but it may be added that some composers (or, in certain cases, their publishers) have introduced a degree of confusion by numbering particular works out of their true chronological order (see the *Oxford Companion to Music*, s.v. 'Opus').

The use of opus numbers is associated by the general public with the performance of what it calls 'classical' music, since the more commonplace compositions are rarely numbered by their makers. On the day this chapter was written the author overheard in the train a conversation illustrating this fact. Two men were arranging together the holding of a suburban concert, and the guiding principle of the construction of the programme was laid down in these words —'No classical music, all good popular stuff—*none of them ops!*'

CHAPTER II

WHAT THE LISTENER REALLY NEEDS TO KNOW

When one comes to think of it, what a lot of musical knowledge there is that does not help the listener—or at least helps him only very indirectly.

One can imagine a keen but ignorant music-lover looking round for something to study. He finds a book called *The Elements of Music*, he masters it, and finds he has got a grasp not of the elements of music at all, but merely of the details of musical notation.

Something more is needed: he inquires and finds that from the *Elements of Music* people often go on to the study of *Harmony*. He buys a text-book, engages a teacher, and finds himself able to string chords together and to write a hymn-tune. But his listening is little more intelligent than before: put the piano score of a symphony before him, and he can spell out the chords and analyse the harmonies, but when the symphony is played he profits little by his new ability. He hears of *Counterpoint*, and takes up that subject: after months of work he can write a tiny exercise, using the technique of the sixteenth-century choral composer. But his listening ability is little increased. The fact is that all this time our poor friend is laboriously acquiring the mere beginnings of the stock-in-trade of a composer (which he will never be), and neglecting to acquire the necessary stock-in-trade of an intelligent listener (which he wishes to be).

What subjects, then, should a listener study? Mainly three—*The Form of Music*, its *History*, and a trifle of *Instrumentation*. And these he should have set out not in the usual text-book manner, for the ordinary text-book of Form goes into details of which he need know nothing, the text-book of History supplies far more dates and names than he will ever require, and the text-book of Instrumentation assumes that its reader wishes to *write* for the orchestra.

To know something of how a piece of music is built will help the listener. To know something of the period in which it was composed, the stage of musical development it represents and the personality of the composer will also help him, and, in the case of an orchestral piece, knowledge of the instruments concerned will give a new interest to his listening.

Knowledge of Form will help him, because it will enable him to detect the musical subject-matter of the piece. As soon as he grasps the fact that a piece of music has definite musical 'Subjects', and is able to identify these and note their treatment, his perception is transformed. What was formerly a puzzling web of sound becomes a clear arrangement of definite 'tunes'—and any one can appreciate a tune. He can now recognize the relation of parts to one another and to the whole. The drawing of the piece is clear to him.

Ability to recognize tone qualities of the various instruments, singly and in combination, makes it possible to observe tonal contrasts he formerly missed. He notes a little theme taken up in turn by the clear-voiced flute, the rich-toned clarinet, and the thin-sounding, piquant oboe. He marvels at the variety of effects of the great body of fiddles, little and big, playing softly or loudly, bowing or plucking their strings, muted or unmuted; he admires the warm tone of the horns playing slow chords. The *colouring* of the piece is now clear to him.

The fact that the composer is not to him a mere name is of importance. He knows something of the joys and sorrows that made up the composer's life, and the piece is no longer a *tour de force* of technical achievement, but a human document, a medium of human expression. The fact that it was written in such-and-such a country enables him to regard it as the expression of a nation, and a period. The knowledge of the position the composer and his national 'school' occupy in the story of musical development enables him to avoid looking for what could not possibly be there—a type of feeling that belongs to a century later, or a manner of composition that belongs to another 'school'.

These three things then are useful: a knowledge of Form, a knowledge of History and Biography, and a simple knowledge of Instrumentation. As for other knowledge, why of course *all* knowledge is of some value, but for the ordinary listener, engaged day after day in weaving or building, in buying or selling, in preaching or teaching, banking or law, a knowledge of these three is all that life will generally allow. And the beauty of it is that, of these three, one, at all events, History and Biography, can become a mere subject of general reading, to be gradually and pleasantly pursued as the days go by, and to be kept up-to-date without effort as new composers appear and articles and books upon them and their works come into one's ken.

CHAPTER III

HOW THE COMPOSER WORKS

Light can be thrown upon the problems of intelligent listening by a little consideration of the problems of composition. It is a truism to say that a piece of music is written to be listened to. It is a piece of self-expression on the part of the composer, but he is expressing himself to someone—to an audience, or to many audiences that will hear his work in many places and at many times, possibly through many centuries. The composer has, then, not merely to express himself, he must do so intelligibly: he must *make himself clear*—and not only this, he must *strike at the feelings* of his hearers. A good sermon is, presumably, a piece of self-expression also, but it is a piece of self-expression aimed at the minds and hearts of a congregation. Neither the piece of music nor the sermon serves its purpose if it simply acts as a safety-valve to the overcharged brain of its writer. It must not be a mere outpouring of thought or emotion; it must be designed for the production of a certain effect.

That very word 'designed' applied to music may startle some simple-minded reader. For, strange as it may seem, there are in the world a number of people who misunderstand the word 'inspiration', and look on the composer as a mere channel—a lightning conductor which collects the electric fluid from the heavens and conveys it to the hearts of men. If these people were to put on paper their picture of a composer at work it would be something like this: A wild-eyed creature, with ruffled hair, seated at an untidy table with music-paper before him, and writing, writing, writing feverishly and excitedly the thoughts that Heaven sends. 'Inspiration' is percolating from the ether into his brain, in burning streams it flows down his arm, into his hand, out at his finger-tips and along his pen, from which it drips over the paper in black-headed crotchets and quavers. The creature rises with a shout of joy—a masterpiece is born!

Or, alternatively, they think of the creature at the piano frenziedly fingering the keys, producing in immediate tone the thoughts that Nature sends him, and then turning to his desk beside him that he may record for after ages the currents and eddies of the afflatus.

Now symphonies do *not* come into the world in this way, any more than do plays, pictures, poems, novels, or cathedrals. Something called inspiration there must be, but something called design also. Of the attempted works of art that fail, some do so from lack of inspiration, and others from imperfection of design or ineffectiveness in its execution. The arts are on an equal footing here, and we can learn something of the methods of work of the composer by considering, for instance, those of the poet. We shall find that 'the poet's eye in a fine frenzy rolling' is an insufficient equipment, and that, in addition, there must be the habits of reflection and calculation, and a readiness to adapt means to ends.

How much of 'inspiration' there may be in the planning of a racing yacht one does not know, but there is certainly something that may go by that name, plus a large amount of calculation. How much of calculation there is in the composition of a poem or symphony is difficult to decide, but there is something that comes under that description, plus a good deal of 'inspiration'.

Amongst those who have lifted the curtain and let the public peep into the room of the poet, Edgar Allan Poe comes first to mind. In his essay on *The Philosophy of Composition* he says:

> 'I have often thought how interesting a magazine paper might be written by any author who would—that is to say, who could—detail, step by step, the processes by which any one of his compositions attained its ultimate point of completion. Why such a paper has never been given to the world I am much at a loss to say—but perhaps the authorial vanity has had more to do with the omission than any one other cause. Most writers—poets in especial —prefer having it understood that they compose by a species of fine frenzy—an ecstatic intuition—and would positively shudder

at letting the public take a peep behind the scenes, at the elaborate and vacillating crudities of thought—at the purposes seized only at the last moment—at the innumerable glimpses of idea that arrived not at the maturity of full view—at the fully matured fancies discarded in despair as unmanageable—at the cautious selections and rejections—at the painful erasures and interpolations—in a word, at the wheels and pinions—the tackle for scene shifting—the step-ladders and demon traps—the cock's feathers, the red paint and the black patches, which, in ninety-nine cases out of the hundred, constitute the properties of the literary *histrio*.'

Having let us into so much of the secret of literary composition, Poe then goes on to analyse the processes by which was brought into existence his poem *The Raven*, prefacing his analysis by these words: 'It is my design to render it manifest that no one point in its composition[1] is referable either to accident or intuition—that the work proceeded step by step to its completion with the precision and rigid consequence of a mathematical problem.' Now Poe had a peculiarly logical and analytical mind. He thought out his processes, and could afterwards account for all he had done, as, probably, few poets can. Some processes of composition which with him were conscious may be with others unconscious; he had reasons where some others have intuitions. But in the case of every successful poet there must be a working to law, more or less conscious, and the principle of design is to be found everywhere throughout the completed work.

It is not difficult in our records of the great composers to find the equivalent of Poe's description of the processes of the poet. Those 'painful erasures', for instance—how well known they were to Beethoven! To him inspiration came, as it came to Poe, as the gifts from above of a mere tiny fragment—with Poe the germ of an idea, with Beethoven just a little handful of notes. And this fragment itself was imperfect, so much so that he turned it over in his mind for months or years, fashioning and refashioning it, polishing and perfecting, and sometimes, after long efforts at improvement, returning

[1] i.e. the work done after the original 'inspiration' had come to him.

finally to an earlier form. He kept beside his very bed a sketch-book in which he could record the musical thoughts which had occurred to him. When he was walking he would stop, and take such a book from his pocket and jot down a new idea that had struck him, or the recasting of an old one. This practice he began as a boy and continued through life, and when he died fifty of his sketch-books which still remained were included in the catalogue of the sale of his effects. His criticism of his own ideas was severe: he discarded many more of his inspirations than he used, so that if he had carried to completion all the symphonies of which his note-books show the beginnings, instead of nine of them, we should have had at least fifty.[1]

> 'The moment he takes his pen in hand he becomes the most cautious and hesitating of men. . . . There is hardly a bar in his music of which it may not be said with confidence that it has been re-written a dozen times. . . . Mendelssohn used to show a correction of a passage by Beethoven in which the latter had pasted alteration after alteration up to 13 in number. Mendelssohn had separated them, and in the 13th Beethoven had returned to the original version.'[2]

Compare the statement of Brahms as to his own processes of composition:

> 'There is no real creating without hard work. That which you would call invention, that is to say, a thought, an idea, is simply an inspiration from above, for which I am not responsible, which is no merit of mine. Yet it is a present, a gift, *which I ought even to despise until I have made it my own by right of hard work.*'

In advising a young composer Brahms said:

> 'It seems to me you are too easily satisfied. . . . Let it rest, let it rest, and keep going back to it and working at it again and again, until it is completed as a finished work of art, until there is not a note too much or too little, not a bar you could improve upon. . . .

[1] M. G. Nottebohm.
[2] Sir George Grove, in his masterly sketch in the *Dictionary of Music and Musicians*.

I am rather lazy, but I never cool down over a work once begun, until it is perfected, unassailable.'[1]

In the case of Beethoven and Brahms the successive stages of composition, the clipping and trimming, the lengthening and shortening of passages, the reshaping of melodies, the recasting of harmonies, and the rebalancing of parts were largely recorded on paper. In the case of some other composers this work has proceeded as a purely mental process, no record being kept. But it has had to be done nevertheless.

'Mozart when he washed his hands in the morning could never remain quiet, but traversed his chamber, knocking one heel against the other immersed in thought. At table he would grasp the corners of his napkin, and while drawing it backwards and forwards on his mouth, make grimaces, apparently lost in meditation.'[2]

Much of Mozart's composition was very rapid, that is to say the actual penning of his work was often quickly achieved. But his mind had been hard at work, accepting and rejecting, and what he produced was the result of the mental labours of a period of this kind superimposed on a basis of long study of the principles of composition.

'It is a very great error to suppose that my art has become so exceedingly easy to me. I assure you that there is scarcely any one who has worked at the study of composition as I have. You could scarcely mention any famous composer whose writings I have not diligently and repeatedly studied throughout.'

This laborious attempt to grasp the principles of effective composition by the study of the great works of others has been made by every great composer. Bach copied out the works of Italian and French composers. Handel travelled much as a young man, hearing and studying the works of other nations. Elgar's awakening came when as a boy he first caught sight of a copy of Beethoven's first symphony, was struck by its effects, and began to study the means

[1] Recorded by Sir George Henschel in *Musings and Memories of a Musician*.
[2] Holmes's standard *Life of Mozart*.

by which these were obtained.[1] His later method of composition was essentially that of Mozart: the labour was done without pen and paper, but it *was* done. As he told the present writer: 'An idea comes to me, perhaps when walking. On return I write it down. Weeks or months after I may take it up and write out the piece of which it has become the germ. The actual labour of writing this, with the complete orchestral scoring, takes perhaps eight or ten hours. But the piece has gradually shaped itself in my mind in the meantime.'

It is interesting to find one recent composer who analysed the processes which he stated to be general amongst composers. This was the French composer, Vincent d'Indy: he based his analysis presumably largely upon a consideration of his own personal experiences, but he based it also upon a long and careful observation of his master and life's friend, the great César Franck. An authentic document of this sort is worth giving at length.

> 'Without going too deeply into technical details, it seems indispensable at this point to remind—or inform—my readers that the creation of any work of art, plastic or phonetic, demands, if the artist is really anxious to express his thoughts sincerely, three distinct periods of work: the conception, the planning out, and the execution.
>
> 'The first, which we have described as the period of conception, is subdivided into two operations: the synthetic and the analytic conception. That signifies for the symphonist the laying down of the broad lines, the general plan of the work, and the determination of its constituent elements—the themes, or musical ideas, which will become the essential points of this plan.
>
> 'These two undertakings generally succeed each other, but are nevertheless connected, and may modify each other in this sense, that the nature of the idea (the personal element) may lead the creative artist to change the order of his preconceived plan; while, on the other hand, the nature of the plan (the element of generality) may invoke certain types of musical ideas to the exclusion of others. But whether it be synthetic or analytic the conception is

[1] See the present Author's *First Book of the Great Musicians*.

always independent of time, place, or surroundings—I had almost added of the artist's will; he must, in fact, wait until the materials from which his work will be built—materials which will account for the form while they are also influenced by it—present themselves to his mind in a completely satisfactory way.

'This mysterious period of conception is sometimes of long duration, especially with the great composers (look at Beethoven's sketch-books), for their artistic consciences compel them to exercise extreme severity in the choice of their utterances, whereas it is the characteristic of second-rate musicians, or those who are infatuated with their own merits, to be satisfied with the first matter which comes to hand, although its inferior quality can only build up a fragile and transient edifice.

'The second period in the creation of a work, which we call the planning out or ordering, is that in which the artist, profiting by the elements previously conceived, definitely decides upon the disposition of his work, both as a whole, and in all its minutest details.

'This work, which still necessitates a certain amount of invention, is sometimes accompanied by long moments of hesitation and cruel uncertainties. It is the time at which a composer undoes one day what it has cost him so much trouble to build up the day before, but it also brings the full delight of feeling himself to be in intimate communion with the Beautiful.

'Finally, when the heart and the imagination have conceived, when the intelligence has ordered the work, comes the last stage, that of execution, which is mere play to a musician who knows his business thoroughly; this includes the actual writing, the instrumentation, if it is required, and the plastic presentation on paper of the finished work.

'If, as regards the general conception and execution of the work, the procedure is more or less identical with all composers, it is far from being uniform in all that concerns the thematic conception and the disposition of the various elements. One musician has to await patiently the blossoming of his ideas; another, on the contrary, will endeavour to force their coming with violence and excitation; a third—like Beethoven—will write in feverish haste an incredible number of different sketches of a single musical thought; a fourth—Bach, for instance—will not give his theme plastic shape until it is absolutely established in his own mind.'[1]

One purpose of this chapter is to destroy wherever it exists the idea that a composer's work is easy—the mere recording of a flow of notes that comes to him from a kindly muse. So far from this work being easy, it is often excessively laborious; the muse gives the man a shilling, with the ability (if he will diligently use it) to turn it into a hundred pounds.

And, that accepted, the way is clear for the next chapter, which gives some idea of the nature of the 'planning' or 'designing' of a piece of music, so far as its general lines are concerned.[2]

[1] Vincent d'Indy's *César Franck* (Mrs. Newmarch's translation, published by John Lane).

[2] Since this chapter was in type I have noticed (what I had long forgotten) that one eminent teacher of musical composition has advised his students to study Poe's essay on literary composition alluded to above. Mr. Frederick Corder, for long Professor of Composition at the Royal Academy of Music, in the introduction to his *Modern Musical Composition: a Manual for Students* (Curwen), says:

'Composition is as much a constructive art as joinery or architecture, and must therefore be practised consciously until long use and experience enable us to exercise our painfully acquired powers subconsciously. Yet nearly every one begins with a vague idea that he has only to turn his eyes to heaven, like a prophet in a picture, to be delivered of a musical work complete in all its parts. I would advise a perusal of Edgar Allan Poe's fine essay on *The Philosophy of Composition* as the most effectual antidote to this pernicious delusion. It is only possible for the long and highly trained expert to dispense with the searchlight of ratiocination, and it is very doubtful whether even he gains anything by so doing. But it is in the nature of the person of feeling to want to do everything by unbridled impulse, as it is in the nature of the intellectual person to love to fill up a form. The real artist—a combination of the two—reasons out his work first; then, having fashioned it in the rough, he re-writes and re-writes until the bare bones are quite hidden. I am aware that cold intelligence and hot enthusiasm are two oddly matched steeds for the chariot of Phoebus Apollo, but they must be taught to go in double harness, neither leading, but side by side and mutually helpful.'

A happy adaptation of Mr. Corder's opening sentence to the special purpose of this book, by the way, might be made as follows: '*Listening* is as much an analytical act as the appreciation of architecture; it must, therefore, be practised consciously until long use and experience enable us to exercise our painfully acquired powers subconsciously.' The succeeding chapters teach *conscious* analysis in listening—in the hope that with many readers this process of analysis will eventually become largely subconscious.

CHAPTER IV

ON THE PRINCIPLE OF DESIGN IN MUSIC

A completed piece of music, then, is not a mere string of notes; it is a piece of intricate design, carefully developed. The composer's whole thought, at frequent intervals, over a long period, has had to be given to his work, lest, by a little too much or too little in one place or another, by a trifling lack of congruity in some of his material, or by some other defect, his labour should be wasted.

Music is human expression, but it is not free expression; it is expression according to rules. These rules are ever changing as the world grows older, but they are always founded on unchanging principles. A young composer, then, needs to know the rules of his game as played in his own period; more important still, he needs to grasp the principles underlying those rules—the spirit behind the letter. If he grasps these principles he may even help to bring into existence new rules.

Does the listener also need to understand those rules and principles? Compare the case of another art. Does the tourist need to understand the rules and principles of architecture? Theoretically, no! The builders wrought to give pleasure to or to inspire devotional feelings in the plain public, and their work should be self-explanatory. Practically, yes! If the tourist knows even a little about the principles of good building, the story of the development of the different styles, and so forth, he will note and enjoy a hundred things over which his eye would otherwise pass unseeing.

Now music is, looked at in one light, architectural, but it is a sort of dream architecture which passes in filmy clouds and disappears into nothingness. You may stand and gaze at a cathedral for a whole morning, and return again and again to study its details. The details of a symphony, on the other hand, are only momentarily before you, and once they are gone cannot be rehearsed until, it may be months later, the same symphony receives a further performance. A knowledge of the rules and principles of composition then helps the hearer by showing him what to expect. Having that knowledge the main lines of the music are clear to him, and his attention can be given to details he would otherwise entirely miss. It would have done Tolstoy a world of good to have had a few lessons in the modern subject of 'Musical Appreciation'. Had he had these he would never have written the following passage:

> 'An acquaintance of yours, a musician of repute, sits down to the piano and plays you what he says is a new composition of his own, or of one of the new composers. You hear the strange, loud sounds, and admire the gymnastic exercises performed by his fingers; and you see that the performer wishes to impress on you that the sounds he is producing express various poetic strivings of the soul. You see his intention, but no feeling whatever is transmitted to you except weariness. The execution lasts long, or at least it seems very long to you, because you do not receive any clear impression, and involuntarily you remember the words of Alphonse Karr, *Plus ça va vite, plus ça dure longtemps*.[1]
>
> 'And it occurs to you that perhaps it is all a mystification; perhaps the performer is trying you—just throwing his hands and fingers wildly about the keyboard in the hope that you will fall into the trap and praise him, and then he will laugh and confess that he only wanted to see if he could hoax you. But when at last the piece does finish, and the perspiring and agitated musician rises from the piano evidently anticipating praise, you see that it was all done in earnest.
>
> 'The same thing takes place at all the concerts with pieces by Liszt, Wagner, Berlioz, Brahms, and (newest of all) Richard Strauss, and the numberless other composers of the new school, who unceasingly produce opera after opera, symphony after symphony, piece after piece.'[2]

[1] The quicker it goes the longer it lasts.
[2] Tolstoy's *What is Art?* (Aylmer Maude's translation). Tolstoy here only says very long-windedly what the man in the train (p. 7) said in four words, 'None of them ops!'

ON THE PRINCIPLE OF DESIGN IN MUSIC

A simple folk-song Tolstoy could understand: a sonata or symphony was beyond him. Tolstoy would abolish all complex music because the plain man cannot grasp it at a sitting. The assumption of the present book is that it is better to abolish the plain man—as a plain man. There is a world of beauty lying just beyond that plain man's reach; it is worth a little striving on his part to find the way to that world and enter in.

Complexity is but simplicity multiplied. The symphony is but the folk-song developed. The forms of all European music boil down to the same simple principle, and that principle can be put in three short words, words so fundamentally true that they would serve equally well, also, for the expression of a national policy or of the basis of a league of nations—*Variety and Unity*. That this principle lies at the root of all formal development in music can be shown by a crude argument of the following kind:

Consider yourself a composer, with the wish to bring into the world a piece of some length—say five minutes or twenty. You are fortunate in that a kind heaven has sent you a happy initial idea, a little tune which you feel to be expressive of something deeply felt within you. Such a tune lasts, perhaps, half a minute (few tunes in themselves last much longer). You write it down, gloat over it with artistic pride, and then say—What next?

Perhaps you decide that the half-minute tune is so good that you will repeat it. You now have a minute-long piece. You can stop there if you like, but it does not seem a very satisfactory thing to do. Then shall you make up your five-minutes 'Song without Words' by ten repetitions of that tiny tune, or your fifty-minute Symphony by one hundred such repetitions? Heaven (which sent you the tune) forbid! No audience would stand it. The best of tunes will outstay its welcome when thus persistent. Such vain repetitions are only permitted in church, where the congregation is so devoutly absorbed in the words of its hymns and psalms that the recurrence of the same tune for many verses passes unnoticed, or amongst the country-folk who so lose themselves in the tale the ballad singer tells that his tune becomes to them its mere vehicle. And you are writing not for church, nor for the bar-parlour of the village inn, but for the concert hall. Mere repetition, then, will not work. You must try another dodge.

This time you put your heaven-sent tune on paper and then wait for heaven to send down another. In an hour or two, or in a few days, it comes—and on to the paper it goes. One and a half or two minutes of your five or your fifty minutes is now provided for. You wait for a third tune, and a fourth and a fifth, and, when they come to you, you add them. At this point it seems wise to try the piece on some friend—or enemy. You find it does not 'go down'. There are two reasons for this. Firstly, there is a certain expenditure of nervous force in enjoying a new tune, and a succession of five different new tunes, straight off the reel, makes too great a call on that nervous force. Secondly, when the thing is done, it sounds not like one thing, but like five. Devise four nice little connecting passages to join up the five tunes and, though improved, still it does not sound a whole.

Your experiments have shown you the truth of the matter. The first one proved to you the necessity of *variety*, the second the necessity of *unity*. You think it all over, and sleep on it before deciding what to do next. It comes to you in a flash when you wake up next morning. Happy thought! You now take your first tune, follow it with your second and *return to your first*. It works! You have hit on the very form of a Mozart Minuet and that in which ninety per cent. of the minuets, short songs, 'Songs without Words', Nocturnes, Dances, and similar delicious trifles are composed. The mind after hearing the first tune (which we will call I) is ready for a change and welcomes the second (which we will call II). After that it does not want further change for the moment, but is ready to welcome again its old friend I.

You now take three of your tunes, which we will call respectively I, II, and III, and arrange them as follows:

$$\text{I II I III I.}$$

That too, you find, is acceptable. You extend this and get:

$$\overbrace{\text{I II I}}\ \text{III}\ \overbrace{\text{I II I.}}$$

Then you have discovered the very plan of a Beethoven Rondo!

I   THE FIRST VIOLINS

II   'CELLOS AND DOUBLE-BASSES

III PICCOLO AND TWO FLUTES

IV FRENCH HORNS

ON THE PRINCIPLE OF DESIGN IN MUSIC

All you need now is to remove any crudities due to your lack of experience in composition. You feel a little dissatisfied still and appeal to a musical friend, who tells you that the feeling of sameness that still remains is due to your three tunes all being in what he calls 'the same key'. Or he points out that they are too similar in 'rhythm'. Or he says that they are too far removed in 'key' or in rhythm, and so forth. But you have at least grasped the right *principle*—Variety and Unity, diversity of material relieved by repetition of material. Your plan will still not reach to the twenty minutes allotted, but you are *on the way* to discover how to write a fifty-minutes' piece. Having found the principle of the Minuet and the Rondo you have found the principle of most European and American music. The problem you have been solving is essentially the very problem of the composer, Beethoven, or Brahms, or Franck, or Elgar, as described in the last chapter. You, however, have merely solved it on broad general lines, and they, with their acutely critical perception, feel called upon to grapple with it over and over again, not only in the general lay-out of their work, but in every one of the details. Ruskin saw this, and used an analogy from music when speaking of pictures:

> 'Take any noble air, and you find, on examining it, that not one even of its faintest or shortest notes can be removed without destruction to the whole passage in which it occurs; and that every note in the passage is twenty times more beautiful so introduced than it would have been if played singly on the instrument. Precisely this degree of arrangement and relation must exist between every touch and line in a great picture. You must consider the whole as a prolonged musical composition.'

CHAPTER V

HOW SMALL INSTRUMENTAL PIECES ARE MADE

Let us see how the principles of the last chapter are applied in some of the smaller masterpieces of popular music. Almost at random we will examine five or six of such masterpieces. If the reader can play them or study their scores, so much the better. If not, the simple reading of this chapter will still help him. The different 'tunes' of the piece are here labelled I, II, &c.

A CHOPIN WALTZ

(The ever-popular one in D flat, Op. 64, No. I.) Here is a diagram of the construction:

I	II	I

I is of a lively 'running' character and lasts for about fifty bars. II is of a more quiet and sustained character, thus making a good contrast. It lasts about thirty bars. Then I returns—'Variety and Unity', in simplest form.[1]

A GRIEG FRAGMENT

The Death of Åse (from the 1st 'Peer Gynt' Suite).

I	II	I	Coda

Here the construction is even simpler, for II is a mere transposition of I into a related key. On the other hand, this piece has a tail or 'Coda', to finish it off. If you play or hear the piece consider the

[1] The technical name for such a form as this is 'Simple Ternary'.

emotional purpose of this 'Coda'. The whole piece is very short, the themes or tunes being each merely eight bars long.

A MACDOWELL PIECE

A.D. 1620 (from the *Sea Pieces*).

| I a | II | . I b | Coda |

As its title implies, this piece is intended to be descriptive of the voyage of the Pilgrim Fathers. It is marked to be played 'In unbroken rolling rhythm', and I evokes images of a sullen sea.

The middle portion, II, has a dignified psalm-like character: on close examination it will be found, however, that its material is somewhat related to that of I, but so treated as to produce a different emotional effect.

When I returns it does so rather in spirit than in body, i.e. it is not slavishly copied, hence the distinction made in the diagram—I *a* and I *b*.

It will be seen that the piece is bound together by the use of a very tiny stock of thematic material, and this material is so variously treated that the piece as a whole, whilst losing nothing in unity, but rather gaining, represents the play of a fairly wide range of emotion. It is much more subtle in construction than the pieces previously mentioned in this chapter, especially in its use of key contrasts, but the formal principle of its construction is just the same.

A CHOPIN NOCTURNE

The favourite one in E flat (Op. 9, No. 2) will serve our purpose here. The general style of the piece (as of its fellow nocturnes) is that of a song in the right hand, with an accompaniment in the left.

| I | I | II | I | II | I | Coda |

The first tune is quite short: on its first appearance it is immediately repeated, so that the main key and the main subject-matter of the piece may be well established in the memory of the hearer. The second tune is also short; it is in the most nearly related key.

It is characteristic of Chopin that at each repetition of his first tune he introduces little changes in the outline of his tune, tiny decorative arabesques in the right-hand part, for instance.

A MENDELSSOHN MARCH

The War March of the Priests. This familiar piece will serve as an example of a simple march form.

| Introduction | I | II | I | III | Interpolation | I | Coda |

The short Introduction, with its drum-rolls and trumpet-call rhythms, establishes the martial atmosphere. It begins softly and increases consistently in loudness and in rhythmic intensity, so-provoking a feeling of expectancy, heralding the first tune and causing it to enter with great effect.

There is a good contrast between the various tunes. I is dignified; II is more restless in feeling; III is a smoothly flowing melody. On its first appearance I is given with repetitions, unnecessary on its subsequent appearances—for reasons already made clear in the case of the previous piece.

The Interpolation near the end serves a similar purpose to the Introduction: it awakens expectancy for the return of the main tune of the piece.

The Coda (which begins with a repetition of part of III, brought into the chief key of the piece, marked to be played loudly instead of softly, and altered in the rhythm of the bass part) provides an effective ending, giving the feeling of climax and finality (compare the same composer's *Cornelius March* with its abrupt close, and see which is the more satisfactory).

A HANDEL AIR WITH VARIATIONS

The Harmonious Blacksmith.[1] Here is a tiny tune, which appears first in all its simplicity, and is then repeated five times, decked out

---

[1] The name is not Handel's, and was not given to the piece until about a century after its composition. It would be correctly described as 'the Air with Variations from the 5th Harpsichord Suite'.

HOW SMALL INSTRUMENTAL PIECES ARE MADE

in various guises. It thus falls into six brief sections, and they might be described as follows:

(*a*) The tune, serene and tranquil.

(*b*) 1st Variation. Proceeding at much the same pace but with a short note interpolated between the notes of the tune itself. Thus in the original tune the notes were chiefly half-beat notes, but here there is a continuous flow of quarter-beat notes in the right hand.

(*c*) 2nd Variation. Like the last but with the quarter-beat notes in the left hand.

(*d*) 3rd Variation. Each beat divided by the right hand into sixths (three plus three). It is not easy at first to say what has become of the tune itself, but one can feel it there. It is like the Cheshire Cat in *Alice in Wonderland*, which disappeared, so far as its material body was concerned, but left behind its characteristic feature, its grin.

(*e*) 4th Variation. Here it is the left-hand part which is divided into sixths of a beat.

(*f*) 5th Variation. The tune is still further disguised, each beat being divided into a rushing scale passage of eight notes, generally in the right hand, but sometimes responded to by a similar rush in the left. This variation brings the piece to a brilliant conclusion.

The general intention of the piece, it will be seen, is to take a simple tune and embellish it, and Handel's emotional plan is one of increasing excitement; beginning with half-beat notes in the tune itself he goes on to quarter-beat notes in Variations 1 and 2, sixth-beat notes in Variations 3 and 4, and eighth-beat notes in Variation 5 The principle of 'Unity and Variety' is obvious enough here, but the formula is different from that used in the pieces formerly explained.

The Air with Variations has been a popular form for centuries. Our English composers invented it in Queen Elizabeth's reign, and by that means did immense service to the progress of the art of composition, since the elaboration of material and the exploration of all its possibilities is a splendid exercise for the ingenuity of composers, and necessarily provides them with a skill in thematic treatment which must help them in all their work. The form exists in all qualities, from the naive twiddlings of the *Home, Sweet Home, with Variations* of commerce, to be had at the music shop of any country town, to the great emotional expressions of Bach, Beethoven, Brahms or Elgar.

NOTE ON 'SIMPLE BINARY FORM'

An early instrumental form, of which many of the shorter pieces of Bach offer good illustrations (e.g. some of his Preludes in the '48', and many of his movements in the Suites and Partitas), is laid out as follows: the piece falls into two halves, which usually begin in much the same way as each other and end in much the same way as each other. The first half, beginning in the main key of the piece, moves away to another (related) key towards its end; the second half, beginning in this other key, moves back to the chief key at its end.

CHAPTER VI

ON THE MYSTERIES OF 'SONATA-FORM'

The term 'Sonata-Form' is one of the most misleading in music. But leave that for the moment, and let us see what the thing is, before discussing its name.

A new feature is now introduced. In the pieces just described[1] the 'tunes' have been for the most part given, on each of their repetitions, in a perfectly straightforward way, and the piece has been in effect a combination of mere tunes, with the possible addition of an Introduction, a brief Interpolation or a Coda. Contrast of Material and Contrast of Key, with Repetition of Material and Repetition of Key, were the means employed to secure artistic effect. The object of 'Variety and Unity' was thus attained.

What may be called the 'emotional plan' of the pieces mentioned was necessarily simple. The 'tunes' themselves might be expressive of various emotional states, and by their alternation emotional variety was secured, but no very subtle play of emotion was possible when we were tied down to a scheme of the presentation of mere short tunes and the repetition of them in their original state, or nearly so.

If the description of the pieces mentioned in the last chapter be read again (and still better, if those pieces be performed or heard) will be found that the one which is much the most flexible in its play of emotion is the 'Sea Piece' of Macdowell. A little thought will show the reason. Its composer has not tied himself down to quite so clear-cut a scheme: he has, for instance, not so much repeated his first tune as produced another passage made out of the same material, using this material in a slightly different way. This has left him free to develop his play of emotions according to his own inner needs—and

[1] With the exception of the Air with Variations.

the word 'develop' is exactly the word that must now be explained.

In the longer modern instrumental forms what is called 'Development' is a most important and valuable artistic device. Essentially it means dismembering a tune and using some of its members in new ways or in new connexions with each other, and generally with a good deal of modulation, i.e. change of key.

What are the 'members' of a tune? Hum the tune of *God save the Queen*. It has seven main divisions, which correspond to the seven lines of the words. Moreover, these main divisions are subdivisible. The first line, for instance, has six notes, and a moment's reflection will reveal that these fall naturally into two subdivisions of three notes each. The six notes sung to *God save our gracious Queen* form a 'phrase' of music; this phrase is divided into two *motifs*[1]—the notes sung to *God save our*, and those sung to *gracious Queen*. When the whole tune has been divided into *motifs* we have reduced it to its lowest rhythmical terms.

Now suppose a composer is writing a *Grand Patriotic Overture* and using our National Anthem as his chief tune. He starts off, let us say, with a flourish of trumpets, as a brief Introduction, and then blares out the tune as it stands, with his full orchestra. After this he has, probably, a little connecting passage (technically called a 'Bridge') leading, say, to *Rule, Britannia* as his second tune,[2] giving us this, for the sake of contrast, in a related key. This portion of the piece, so far as we have got, is called the 'Exposition' or 'Enunciation'. From a formal point of view, its function is to 'expose' or 'enunciate' the themes on which the piece is to be made.

The composer now wants something a little less plain-sailing than either of his two tunes as it stands, so he proceeds to 'develop' *God save the Queen*. He takes (say) that first *motif* and writes a passage in which the *motif* is repeated over and over again, rising a note each time, and getting louder every time—thus working up the excitement of the audience. Or he writes a passage in which it is repeated, sinking a note lower every time—thus calming down the excitement of

[1] Pronounce *Moteef*.

[2] American readers may substitute *The Star-Spangled Banner* for *Rule, Britannia* as the second tune. *God save the Queen* can still stand as the first tune, under its American title of *My Country, 'tis of Thee*.

the audience. Or he tosses that *motif* from one instrument of the orchestra to another. Or he repeats it several times at different pitches, with different harmonies, which results in taking us rapidly through different keys, related and unrelated, and so in producing in our minds a happy feeling of unexpectedness and 'never-know-what-next-ness'.

He also uses one or two other lines or *motifs* of this first tune in a similar way, and then gives us a passage similarly 'developed' from the second tune. At last, perhaps (happy thought), he manages to contrive a brilliant passage in which parts of the two tunes are heard together in different instruments of the orchestra.[1]

Such devices as these constitute 'Development', and when the audience may be thought to have had enough of it, the composer comes back to the repetition (or 'Recapitulation') of his first tune and of his second tune pure and simple, and then with a brilliant, dashing Coda ends his *Grand Patriotic Overture*, amidst the applause of an excited audience.

One proviso must be made. On its first appearance *Rule, Britannia* was heard not in the main key of the piece, but in a related key. On its second appearance, so near the end of the piece, it will be necessary for it to appear in the main key of the piece so that the 'tonality' or 'main-key-ness' of the piece may be well established at the close.

The plan of the *Grand Patriotic Overture* just composed is then as follows:

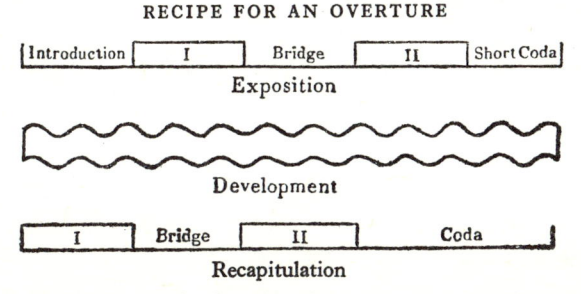

RECIPE FOR AN OVERTURE

| Introduction | I | Bridge | II | Short Coda |

Exposition

Development

| I | Bridge | II | Coda |

Recapitulation

This *Grand Patriotic Overture* is a very unassuming piece of

[1] *God save the Queen* is a three-beat rhythm and *Rule, Britannia* is a two-beat rhythm, but he has a choice of several simple means of adjusting this.

32 ON THE MYSTERIES OF 'SONATA-FORM'

musical expression, popular patriotism being one of the most ingenuous and least subtle of emotional states. Let us now take any well-known sonata-form piece which aims at deeper expression, and, reversing the synthetical process just indulged in, try our hand at analysis. Suppose we choose the first section (or 'Movement') of Beethoven's celebrated *Pathetic Sonata* (Op. 13). Most pianists know this, so the reader can either play it himself or get it played to him. And if he can do neither, he will still be able to follow the analysis here given.[1]

BEETHOVEN'S 'PATHETIC' SONATA. THE FIRST MOVEMENT ANALYSED

Exposition. Introduction of 10 bars. Slow and movingly powerful. Constructed entirely from one little strongly rhythmic *motif*, developed with great skill.

First Subject (Bars 11–27), agitated. Key C minor.

Bridge (Bars 27–51), partly contrapuntal, on material taken from First Subject.

Second Subject (Bars 51–121), falling into two parts (51–89 and 89–121). Prevailing keys E flat minor and E flat major, with, of course, transient passages through other keys. The two parts of this subject are so distinct that to some hearers they may appeal as two different subjects.

Small Coda—or Codetta (Bars 121–32) made out of material of First Subject.

At this point Beethoven directs that everything so far performed shall be repeated. His 'Exposition' or presentation of his themes having been made he wishes, apparently, to make sure of their impression on his hearers' minds.[2] After this he interpolates, with great effect, a four-bars' reminiscence of his solemn Introduction, and then proceeds to the

Development (Bars 139–96). This will be found to be made of *motifs*

[1] If studying this with a copy of the Sonata, number the bars, beginning with the first.

[2] Such a repetition of the Exposition is almost invariable in the older Sonatas and Symphonies.

ON THE MYSTERIES OF 'SONATA-FORM'

taken from the First Subject and the Bridge. It is comparatively short, and less fully worked out than is often the case with Beethoven.

Recapitulation. First Subject (Bar 197 onwards), Key C minor as before, slightly altered at end so as to lead to another key, and trailing off into a short

Bridge.

Second Subject (Bars 223–87) made up of the same two tunes as before, but this time in the keys of F minor and C minor.

Coda (Bars 287 to end) made from material of First Subject with a brief Interpolation from Introduction.

It will be seen that if we were to set out this analysis in diagrammatic form the result would be essentially the same as that recorded in the case of the *Grand Patriotic Overture* imagined earlier in the chapter. But there is a wealth of detail in the Beethoven piece which cannot be recorded diagrammatically. The bold harmonies and daring modulations, the subtle resemblances of the material used in the Introduction and in the First Subject and Second Subject (so unobtrusive as to be unnoticed by many hearers and players, and yet sufficient to bind the piece together in a wonderfully effective way), the interpolation at two places in the piece of definite allusions to the Introduction with which it opened (again binding the piece together as a whole), and many other details of form deserve close examination on the part of any readers who have a really serious interest in the subject. Such examination is, however, not necessary on the part of the ordinary hearer, whose purpose is served if he has been enabled to identify the principal subjects and to recognize them on their reappearances, and, being familiar with these subjects, to follow a little of their treatment in the Development portion of the piece. Even so much ability will transform a mere hearer into an intelligent listener, and will add tenfold to the pleasure of a concert. The mystery of 'Sonata Form' is no great mystery at all!

In the previous chapter there was given an illustration of the form of a simple Rondo. There is also a rather more complex Rondo form called Sonata-Rondo Form. There is no need to explain it here as this is not a text-book of Musical Form, intended for serious students of music and would-be composers. From the listener's point of view it is sufficient to say that this form is a combination of the features of the form of Simple Rondo with some of those of Sonata-form, embodying a good deal of 'development'. If the hearer can identify the 'Subjects', or tunes, his listening will be intelligent.

CHAPTER VII

ON THE SONATA OR SYMPHONY AS A WHOLE

We are now in a position to examine a Sonata or Symphony as a whole, and the simplest thing to say is that such a piece is a combination of three or four shorter pieces strung together to make one long one. That is not a complete definition, and, moreover, by no means every piece that could be so described is a Sonata or Symphony, but the description will serve our purpose if we add that the words Sonata or Symphony cannot be applied to anything light or trivial, but imply some serious expression of human feeling, not necessarily solemn, but with a certain quality of depth.

The various pieces that make up a Sonata or Symphony are technically called 'Movements', perhaps from the fact that they necessarily contrast with one another in speed, a slow piece following a quicker one, and being in turn followed by a quicker one, and so forth. It will generally be found that one or more of the 'Movements' is in the form described in Chapter VI, and that explains the title 'Sonata Form' there used. It is an unfortunate term, as logically 'Sonata Form' ought to be the plan of the Sonata *as a whole*.

When this form of piece is composed for one instrument (as piano) or for two (as for piano and violin) it is called a 'Sonata': when it is written for full orchestra it is called a 'Symphony'. Most of the classical and the longer modern instrumental Trios, Quartets, and Quintets are simply Sonatas for three, four, and five instruments respectively. A Concerto is really nothing but a Symphony or Sonata for one chief solo instrument with full orchestra.

It will perhaps be helpful to take a few examples of well-known Sonatas and Symphonies and to summarize their constitution. In this way we can gather the general characteristics of such pieces.

BEETHOVEN'S 'PATHETIC' SONATA (Op. 13)

The piece consists of three contrasted movements.

1st Movement. Intense and tragic in character, slow Introduction followed by agitated Movement proper—in 'Sonata Form' (see Chapter VI).

2nd Movement. Calmer in character; slow and gentle but deeply expressive. A great contrast to the previous movement. The form is that of a simple Rondo, I, II, I, III, I, Coda. It is the general emotional character of this movement which perhaps justifies the name 'Pathetic' as that of the Sonata as a whole. (The name was given by the composer himself.)

3rd Movement. A rapid, restless piece in Rondo Form.[1]

BEETHOVEN'S 'MOONLIGHT' SONATA (Op. 27, No. 2)

Beethoven did not call this by the above name, now so often given to it, but simply styled it 'Sonata quasi una Fantasia', indicating, by those words, that he had written not a mere piece of chilly classical perfection, but something with freedom and throbbing life. There are, again, three movements.

1st Movement. A romantic song-without-words style of piece, slow and sustained. There is no need for the listener to analyse the form of a piece like this, which makes its own effect at a first

[1] Some of the many amateur pianists who play this sonata may like to analyse it in detail, there being a natural human instinct that prompts a child to take its toy engine to pieces to see how it works, and that, similarly, suggests to an intelligent adult the analysis of a work of art, A general guide to the analysis of the First Movement will be found in Chapter VI, and to that of the Second Movement, above. As for the Third Movement, the rough lines of the analysis are as follows (the bars should be marked throughout, counting the first incomplete bar as one):—I, C minor (bar 1); Bridge (bar 19): II, E flat major (bar 26); Bridge (bar 44): I (bar 62): III, A flat major (bar 79); Bridge (bar 108): I (bar 121); Bridge (bar 129): II, this time transposed to key C major (bar 135); Bridge (bar 154): I (bar 172): Coda (bar 183). Remember that the details of analysis are often debatable. The two great things to notice are the skilful contrivance of the scheme of keys and alternations and contrast of the subjects. Ask yourself in what ways the form of this piece differs from 'Sonata Form'. Having laid out the main lines, look for a lot of detail which cannot be indicated here; in fact, study every bar of the piece. Note whether material used in 'Bridges' and elsewhere is new or whether it is founded on what has appeared before.

ON THE SONATA OR SYMPHONY AS A WHOLE 37

hearing. It is noticeable, indeed, that a strict analysis according to any received formula is almost impossible. Yet the principle of 'Unity and Variety' is evident, and the form is roughly 'Ternary' (first part, second part, first part again).

2nd Movement. A pleasant Minuet and Trio, with a dash of deeper emotion than the name of a mere dance-form would suggest. The Minuet and Trio often appear as one of the movements of a Sonata or Symphony. As the Minuet is played first, followed by the Trio, which in turn is followed by the Minuet again, the form of the whole is that 'Ternary' form which we found in Chapter V to be so common in short pieces of music. If this Minuet be examined separately it will be seen to be itself in 'Ternary' Form. (The word 'Trio' of course means a piece of three lines of music throughout, as one for three instruments, or voices. As used in the Sonata or Symphony the word is often a mere relic and a misnomer; the 'Trio' is simply another Minuet, placed here to contrast with the first one, and to form the middle 'subject' of I, II, I, or 'Ternary' form).

3rd Movement. A very virile, rapid piece, in Sonata Form, with a long and brilliant Coda.

BEETHOVEN'S 'SONATA WITH THE FUNERAL MARCH'
(Op. 26)

1st Movement. A beautifully expressive Air with Variations.

2nd Movement. A 'Scherzo' with Trio, and then Scherzo repeated (simple 'Ternary' form again). The Minuet, and Trio, as already explained, were a common feature as a middle movement in the earlier Sonatas and Symphonies: Beethoven in many cases quickened the speed beyond the possibilities of the dance from which the original form of the movement was derived, introduced unexpected turns of harmony, melody, and rhythm, occasionally abandoned the Minuet's three-in-a-bar rhythm, and gave the whole a boisterous humour which justified the word 'Scherzo' (=a joke).

3rd Movement. 'Funeral March on the Death of a Hero' (simple

Ternary form, with a very brief Coda). What a contrast to the preceding movement!

4th Movement. A rippling piece, in Sonata-Rondo form.

BEETHOVEN'S 'EROICA' SYMPHONY (No. 3 of his nine Symphonies, and Opus 55)

1st Movement. A bold first subject on the simplest little doh-me-soh chord possible, and a long and well-worked-out second subject. The 'Development' portion is very extensive, and embodies some wonderful strokes of genius in the way of display of varied emotions: 'unexpectedness' is a feature. This movement is twice as long as the corresponding movement in the two symphonies previously written by the composer.

2nd Movement. 'Funeral March.' A piece of deeply-felt musical expression. As regards form it is on the Simple Ternary plan, but extended by processes of development throughout. At the very end a fragment of the main theme of the piece appears broken, as it were, with sobs—a very moving effect.

3rd Movement. Scherzo and Trio. A fine, long, vivacious movement, in which much depends on the effect of delicate, very soft playing of rapid passages.

4th Movement. After a few bars of rushing scales and heavy chords there begins an Air with Variations on a very original plan—perhaps most simply described as variations *on two airs*. The first air appears and submits to two variations; then comes the second air, the first now appearing as the bass to the second. Other variations of a most ingenious and effective kind follow.

In 1802, his first two symphonies having been written, Beethoven said to a friend: 'I am not satisfied with my symphonies up to the present time. From to-day I mean to take a new road.' The new road led him to this long and elaborate work. The forms of the movements are the same as those used in previous works, but the emotional content is immeasurably greater. The first title of the work was *Buonaparte*, but on hearing that the hero to whom the piece was dedicated had been proclaimed Emperor, Beethoven indignantly tore

ON THE SONATA OR SYMPHONY AS A WHOLE 39

off the title-page of his manuscript, and he later substituted the present title followed by the significant words 'composed to celebrate the *memory* of a great man' (the italics are ours, not Beethoven's).

It took the symphony nine years to arrive at an English performance and twenty years to arrive at a French one, the reason undoubtedly being the state of scare into which many people are thrown by the hearing of anything novel in style. The forms of the symphony are, as above stated, those previously usual; but they are treated with a new freedom and elaborated to unheard-of length, and conductors in England and France probably feared that the public would be unable to grasp the logic of so long-winded and involved a piece. The incident is in itself an illustration of the need of such instruction in the principles of composition from the listener's point of view as this book tries in its elementary way to give. If the reader will gain a grasp of the *principles* of musical form, as outlined here, and will diligently exercise himself in the art of attentive listening, he will be much less in danger of bewilderment than he would otherwise be on occasions when something startlingly new is announced for performance. For the most outrageous modernities of musical art are generally found to respect the same old main laws of musical being, and the ability to grasp and remember subjects gained by careful listening to Beethoven will help one to a comprehension of Bartók. Of the Sonata in the hands of both Beethoven and Bartók one may say, 'It is all triumphant art, but art in obedience to laws.'[1]

One curious point may have struck the reader in considering the general schemes of the works outlined above. Everywhere the design or 'form' of any particular 'movement' is logical, but the symphony or sonata as a whole seems to have no design or form, but to be a mere string of pieces—a sort of piano recital or orchestral concert programme made up by the inclusion of three or four pieces in deliberate contrast to one another. In other words, it is open to argument whether Beethoven's *Heroic Symphony*, outlined above, is one piece or four. In answer to this it may be said that there is, firstly, a connexion of key between the different movements. A symphony or sonata begins and ends in the same key, and the middle movements

[1] Browning, *Abt Vogler*.

are generally in keys that we feel to be 'related'. Secondly, it may be said that there is, or ought to be, a connexion of style and of feeling. Thirdly, it may be added that, in some cases at all events, there is a resemblance of subject-matter—though where it occurs in the pieces mentioned above it is generally not so obvious that one is inclined to think it conscious on the part of the composer.[1]

Despite these threads of connexion, it is, frankly, an arguable point whether such works are actually artistic 'wholes', and whether in accepting them as such we are not more influenced by convention and old usage than by our critical artistic sense.

The more modern composers seem to have felt as a defect the looseness of connexion between movements, and it is common to-day to bind together the movements by the use of some amount of actual common material. Let us take Elgar's magnificent First Symphony as an example. Its plan is somewhat as follows:

ELGAR'S SYMPHONY IN A FLAT

1st Movement. Slow impressive Introduction, followed by quick movements—often very sad, and frequently strenuously heart-searching, but with a triumphant ending.

2nd Movement. A sort of Scherzo, with many changes of mood.

3rd Movement. A sincerely-felt deeply emotional slow piece.

4th Movement. Slow Introduction followed by a very elaborate and finely-conceived quick movement.

Stated as above, there would seem to be little divergence from the Beethoven plan, and indeed the Symphony *is* a Beethoven symphony (*a*) for a bigger orchestra and (*b*) with an extension of Beethoven's tendency to substitute a group of two or three tunes for the single tune used as a 'subject' in earlier works, and (*c*) with modern feeling. But when one comes to hear the piece or to read the score one feels at once a greater unity, and on examination it will be seen that this is obtained by a certain community of thematic material throughout the work. The slow introductory tune of the first movement is

[1] A careful examination will show resemblances of this kind in the *Pathetic Sonata* and the *Heroic Symphony*.

discovered to be what has been called a 'central theme'. It begins the first movement and ends the last, and there are references to it here and there throughout the work. It is not merely a formal link, but a link of thought and feeling too. One feels that the symphony grows out of that germ. Then again, the main themes of the second and third movements are really the same theme in two different forms, and those movements are, significantly, marked to be played without any break between them. And there are other connexions. In the Beethoven Symphony or Sonata, we may say that *each movement* was organic: in the Elgar Symphony *the whole work* is organic. And this binding together of a whole work is undoubtedly a characteristic of musical art to-day. Wagner, by a somewhat similar device, made his opera scores one consistent whole.

In closing this chapter a word of advice may be given about the use of the annotated programmes commonly sold in the concert hall. This species of literature was introduced by John Ella in connexion with his concerts during the forties and fifties of last century. If we are not mistaken he had the books delivered to the subscribers' houses *in advance of the concert*, and advance study of such literature is the only valuable study. If in a quiet hour the day before the concert, by a study of the music-type examples in the programme book, you can get the themes into your head, with an idea of their treatment, by all means do so. If, however, you can buy the book only a minute or two before the performance begins, far better not try to follow its analysis, which is almost always technical in its terms, involved in its arrangement, and, when hastily read, altogether productive of a wrong state of mind. Glance at any particulars of a literary basis to the piece (which often exists), note the number and order of movements, and then leave the programme on your lap, trust to your ears, and get as much enjoyment out of the new work as your own unaided intelligence and your more or less musical nature will permit—writing off the rest as a bad debt.

It would be a pity if anything written in this or the preceding chapters led any reader to make a fetish of form. Form is merely one of the *means* of a composer, and to be aware of his means enables one often to understand his end. But the Music's the thing!

CHAPTER VIII

'WHAT DO YOU MEAN BY YOUR MOUNTAINOUS FUGUES?'

That was the question Browning asked of Master Hugues—and it is the question many a listener has asked before and since.

For the appreciation of the fugue is the 'acid test' of musical appreciation. Can a man understand a fugue? Admit him at once to the honourable company of intelligent listeners; he must perforce have the root of the matter in him.

'See, the church empties apace,' says Browning as he plays his fugue, and there is, indeed, nothing so effectual at clearing out the congregation. 'A fugue', says some American humorist,[1] 'is a piece in which the voices one by one come in and the people one by one go out.'

That, by the way, gives us a clue to the vital secret of fugue appreciation—a fugue is a piece in 'voices', and these must be listened for. It may be an instrumental piece, but still we speak of it as being in two 'voices', or (more commonly) three, four, or five 'voices'. Fugue is, therefore, originally and essentially, a choral form. Whether composed for choir or for organ, harpsichord, piano, string quartet or orchestra, in the fugue we find a certain number of 'parts' or 'voices' maintained pretty strictly throughout. In other words, a fugue is a piece of woven fabric with a certain number of threads running through it. In a Sonata or Symphony you may find a momentary use of this weaving process; in the Fugue it is consistently employed throughout. The Fugue is Counterpoint *in excelsis*.[2]

[1] Quoted by Surette and Mason in *The Appreciation of Music*. A similar description of a fugue was given to Schumann by someone—'a composition in which one voice rushes out before another, and the listener, first of all' (*see* Hadow, *Studies*, vol. i, p. 177).

[2] See definition of 'Counterpoint' in Chapter I.

MOUNTAINOUS FUGUES

The next secret is this—the Fugue is made out of a 'Subject'. So were the Sonata and Symphony movements, so were the March and Nocturne and Air with Variations mentioned in a previous chapter. But the Subjects of these latter were quite long, fully organized, harmonized 'tunes', and the Fugue Subject is a mere snatch of melody—a bar or two of a simple line of notes such as could, without much difficulty, be played with one finger.

Consider the Sonata and the Fugue as sermons. The Sonata-sermon begins with a reading of two long passages (two parables, say, or two incidents from Scripture) which are thrown into contrast with each other at the outset (Exposition), discussed in detail (Development), and then re-read in the light of the treatment they have just received (Recapitulation). The Fugue-sermon, on the other hand, is a thoughtful exegesis of a single fragmentary 'text'—a mere few words of Holy Writ.

So far, then, we have got to this point—a Fugue is in so many voices, and it is founded on a fragment of melody, called a 'Subject'. A third characteristic must now be made clear. Each voice enters in its turn[1] with the 'Subject', alternating from one key to another (e.g. first voice, Subject in key C; second voice, Subject in key G; third voice, Subject in key C again). We call the responsive entries in another key (the 'dominant key') by the name 'Answer'.

That is how the piece opens, and Browning puts it clearly enough in his famous description:

> First you deliver your phrase
> —Nothing propound, that I see,
> Fit in itself for much blame or much praise—
> Answered no less, where no answer needs be:
> Off start the Two on their ways.
>
> Straight must a Third interpose,
> Volunteer needlessly help;
> In strikes a Fourth, a Fifth thrusts in his nose,
> So the cry's open, the kennel's a-yelp,
> Argument's hot to the close.

[1] Hence the humorous definition already quoted.

There is the 'Exposition' of a Fugue. It corresponds with the Exposition of a Sonata. It is the first section of the piece, and in it the listener's business (if the phrase may be allowed) is, as in the Sonata, to acquaint himself with the musical material out of which the piece is to be constructed. He must grasp the 'Text' or he will be lost in the 'Sermon'.

Now the old rule of 'Variety and Unity' comes into force in the Fugue, as in every piece of music, and as variety we have a short passage, happily called an Episode, after which we are prepared to return to our Subject. But right through our study of Form we have found that variety in music has a double meaning, variety of *material* (or of its treatment) and variety of *key*. The Episode gives us variety of material or of treatment of material; it also leads us (or 'modulates') into another key. This done, the Subject enters, in one or two, or (it may be) all the voices, in that key. It would appear as though Browning is describing the first episode of a Fugue in the verse that follows those already given:

> One dissertates, he is candid;
> Two must discept—has distinguished;
> Three helps the couple, if ever yet man did;
> Four protests; Five makes a dart at the thing wished:
> Back to One, goes the case bandied.

'Back to One, goes the case bandied' alludes to the re-entry of the Subject after the Episode. In Browning's particular imaginary Fugue it is the same voice which first sang the Subject in the Exposition that sings it again in the second group of entries: actually it might be that voice or any other.

Then comes another Episode, with its modulation to still another key, followed by another Entry, or group of Entries in that key, which is in turn followed by another Episode, and so on till the end —Variety and Unity, obtained by skilful changes and repetition of both key and material. And as regards thematic material let it be said that almost invariably the Episodes of a Fugue are constructed (by a process akin to some forms of 'development' in a Sonata) from the already existing musical ideas of the piece—some few notes of the Subject, for instance, perhaps imitatively in the various voices. So though there is *variety* of treatment, there is, throughout the piece, *unity* of material and style.

And that is a Fugue! A Fugue may have lots of other devices, but if a piece fulfils the conditions outlined above it is a Fugue. There are even Fugues (and famous ones) which do not quite fulfil those conditions. The very first Fugue of Bach's '48' has no Episodes, but is merely a string of entries, one after the other.

Let us now consider some of the less essential but still frequent and even usual devices of Fugue form.

'COUNTER-SUBJECT'

In many Fugues when the second voice enters with the Subject (now called 'Answer') the first voice takes up not a mere string of accompanying notes but an actual little tune called a 'Counter-subject'. Then, when the third voice enters, the second voice takes the Counter-subject, and so forth. A simple diagram of the Exposition of a five-part Fugue will make this clear. We will suppose that the highest voice opens, and that the Fugue is in key C.

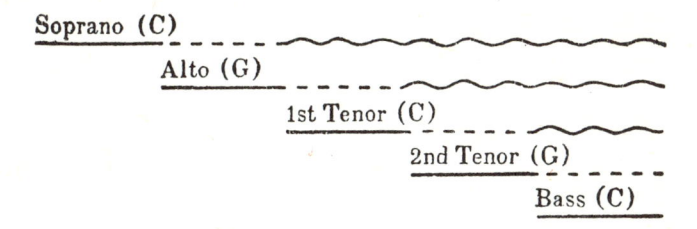

Soprano (C) ─ ─ ─ ─ ～～～～～～～～～～
   Alto (G) ─────── ─ ─ ─ ─ ～～～～～～～
      1st Tenor (C) ─────── ─ ─ ─ ─ ～～～
         2nd Tenor (G) ─────── ─ ─ ─ ─
            Bass (C) ───────

Here the solid line indicates the Subject (or Answer), the dotted line the Counter-subject,[1] and the wavy line the mere contrapuntal continuation with which the voices keep themselves out of mischief once they have delivered themselves of their actual message.

Just to make sure we understand an Exposition let us make another diagram, this time a four-part Fugue in key E.

[1] There is no word 'Counter-answer', though logically there ought to be.

Soprano (B)
Alto (E)
Tenor (B)
Bass (E)

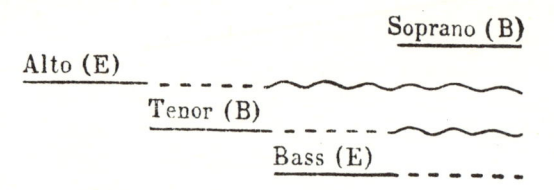

STRETTO

In many Fugues some entries of the subject overlap one another in this way—

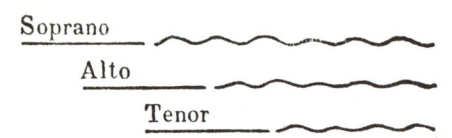

Soprano
Alto
Tenor

This device is called 'stretto' (meaning 'drawn together'), and it is an obvious means of piling up excitement. Stretti usually occur near the end of a Fugue, but there was no binding Bach to text-book regulations, and the very first Fugue of his '48' (already mentioned) is full of stretti throughout.

PEDAL

A thrilling effect is sometimes obtained when the organist, by the composer's direction, places his foot on a low note and keeps it booming there whilst his fingers wander rapidly over the keys, playing the upper voices of the score. This device of a momentarily stationary 'voice' is called 'pedal', and even when the device is used in a piano, orchestral or choral Fugue, the same name is applied.

Whole books can be and have been written on Fugue, but the information given above is sufficient for the listener. He knows now what to expect, and as one's expectations have a great deal to do with one's enjoyment, it is to be hoped he will find the chapter helpful.

The thing now is to play, or get a friend to play, some of Bach's Piano or Organ Fugues, exercising oneself in the detection of the subject whenever it appears, and noting as much as possible any other features of the piece. When enough practice in intelligent listening has been put in for one to do most of this work subconsciously, and to give oneself to the emotional content of the work (for despite its ingenious construction a good Fugue *is* emotional), then one has become a perfect listener. If the friendly pianist or organist is not to be found, then perfection in the art of listening to Fugues may not be so easy of attainment, but you will still find your understanding an appreciation increased by the mere fact that you now know that (*a*) a Fugue is a piece in *Voices*, (*b*) that it is founded upon a tiny melodic *Subject*.

Many set Fugues are preceded by a piece of an introductory nature, generally styled a PRELUDE, usually a movement developed from a single musical idea or *motif*.

It may just be said before leaving the subject that short passages in Fugue style (called 'Fugato') are not uncommon in Sonata and Symphonies. One of the Variations in the last movement of the Beethoven Symphony, explained in the last chapter, is a bit of freely written Fugato.

CHAPTER IX

ON 'PROGRAMME MUSIC'

Here again is a rather foolish term; it is one that is perfectly understood by the musician, but, as experience shows, quite puzzling to the layman. Illustrating this, the writer has found a strong disposition on the part of the smaller printers whenever they find the words 'Programme Music' in a lecture report or article to interpolate the word 'of'. 'Programme of Music' the country compositor can understand; 'Programme Music' means nothing to him.

'Programme Music' is a term loosely applied to any piece which is of the nature of definite musical illustration of a scene or event, or of a series of thoughts or emotions. In other words it is music with

ON 'PROGRAMME MUSIC' 49

a strong pictorial or dramatic leaning, and its effects are rather towards representation than towards formal beauty. It is difficult to arrive at an exact definition, but, the idea will have been grasped from the above explanation.

A very simple, old-fashioned piece of Programme Music for Piano and Violin is before the writer at the moment. It is briefly described by its composer as a

> 'Grand Miscellaneous, Curious, and Comical Piece of Music . . . in which is introduced the DOWNFALL OF PARIS, the whole concluding with a New and Joyful Piece of Music composed for the Occasion call'd THE DEFINITIVE TREATY, and the Restoration of France, or Peace Proclaimed between TWO GREAT NATIONS, Announced by the Sound of Trumpets, Bells ringing, playing merry peals, and the firing of the Guns most respectfully inscribed to the British Ladies by Signor Lampieri. Price 2/6.'

By an ingenious combination of the arts the British Ladies are left in no doubt as to the 'programme' of ideas intended to be illustrated in the piece, the date of which appears to be 1815. The following, for instance, is clear enough:

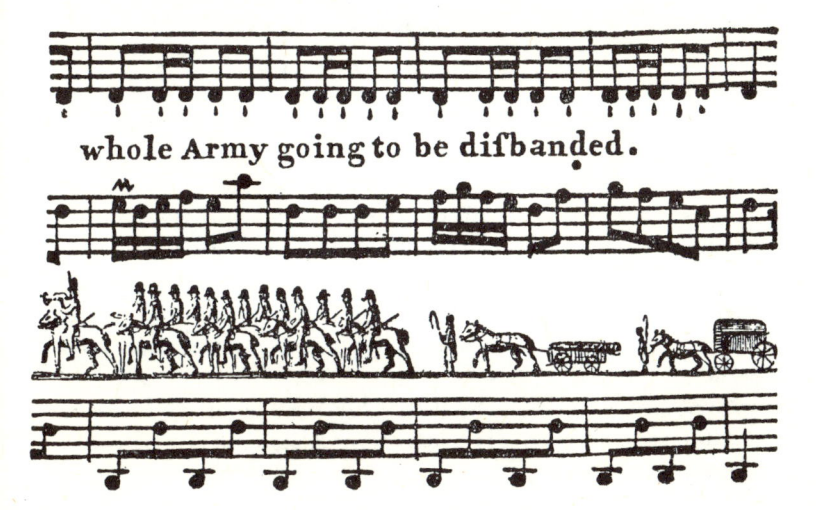

whole Army going to be disbanded.

The whole 'programme' of events includes such features as 'Thanksgiving', described by sixteen bars of bustling semi-quavers, 'Ringing of the Bells', a 'Peal' ('a little in discord to give more effect'), and, as already shown, a happy 'Retreat of the whole Army going to be disbanded'.

The performers are sometimes called on to produce mighty strokes of imitative effort, as for instance in the following:

Now that is 'Programme Music'—at its crudest, the instruments being asked for the most part to *imitate sounds*. Such imitation will also be found in Beethoven's *Pastoral Symphony*, where the song of the cuckoo and the nightingale and the roar and crash of the thunderstorm are brought to the hearers' recollection by an attempt at their reproduction on the orchestra. Beethoven's effort is of a higher order than that of the good Signor, because Beethoven has not merely reproduced sounds, but has at the same time made some really good music.

More legitimate, however, than a 'programme' of the imitation of natural or other sounds is a dramatic programme of representation of *emotions*. Even here, however, the music cannot be considered as one of the very highest forms of art, since it cannot, to be fully appreciated, stand alone, and either a descriptive title or an actual literary 'programme' has to be prefixed to he piece, in order that it may be completely understood and make its full effect.

Liszt defined such a literary 'programme' as:

'Any foreword in intelligible language added to a piece of pure instrumental music, by which the composer intends to guard the hearer against an arbitrary poetic interpretation, and to direct his attention in advance to the poetical idea of the whole, or to a particular part of it';

and he adds:

'The programme has no other object than to indicate preparatively the spiritual moments which impelled the composer to create his work, the thoughts which he endeavoured to incorporate in it.'[1]

Liszt's published 'programme' to his pieces often consisted of a lengthy Preface, or sometimes of a poem. His *Ce qu'on entend sur la montagne*[2] is based on one of Hugo's *Les Feuilles d'Automne*, and the whole poem is printed at the beginning of the score. His *Les Préludes* is preceded by a sort of prose summary of the thought of one of Lamartine's *Méditations poétiques*. His *Hamlet* and his *Hungaria* have no printed 'programme', it being thought, probably, that the very titles are sufficient to give the listener the clues needed.

Let us look at some other instances of Programme Music. The little Macdowell *Sea Piece* mentioned in Chapter V has its main thought suggested by its title, *A.D. 1620*. An imaginative brain at once begins to think of mighty seas, rock-bound coasts, the cockle-shell *Mayflower*, Puritan heroism, psalm-singing, and the like. And once that order of ideas has been set going each can easily interpret the piece in his own way (which may in detail be a little different

---

[1] See Professor Niecks's standard work, *Programme Music in the last Four Centuries: a Contribution to the History of Musical Expression* (Novello), for a full discussion of the aims of Liszt and the other programmists. The present chapter is necessarily a good deal indebted to Professor Niecks's able historical exposition of the whole subject.

[2] *What one hears on the mountain.*

from that of his neighbour), and so get the pleasure of fine music, combined with some of the pleasure of poetry. Strauss's *Tod und Verklärung*[1] and César Franck's *Le Chasseur maudit*[2] have programmes prefixed, Saint-Saëns's *Danse macabre* has a poem. Fully to appreciate Elgar's *Froissart* Overture one should be acquainted with a passage in Scott's *Old Mortality*, and, to some extent, with Froissart also. Tchaikovsky's *Romeo and Juliet* and *The Tempest* take for granted the listener's acquaintance with Shakespeare, and the latter has an actual 'programme' attached (The sea. Ariel, an airy spirit obeying the will of the magician Prospero. . . . Wreck of the ship bringing Ferdinand, &c.).

Tchaikovsky's definition of Programme Music was as follows:

'In the narrower sense this word signifies such symphonic music, or such instrumental music generally, as illustrates a definite subject placed before the public in a programme, and as bears the title of the subject.'

He added:

'I find that the inspiration of a composer can be of two kinds: subjective and objective. In the former case he expresses his personal feelings of joy and sorrow in the music, just as the lyric poet, so to speak, pours out his soul in poems. Here the programme is not only unnecessary, but impossible. It is otherwise when the musician is reading a poetic work, or at the sight of a beautiful landscape is inflamed by enthusiasm to musically characterize the subject that fills him with ecstasy. In this case a programme is indispensable.'

He goes on to say that, in his judgement, it is a pity that Beethoven did not provide a 'programme' to certain of his sonatas, and this, by the way, recalls the statement of Beethoven himself to one of his friends that in composing he had a picture before his mental eye.[3]

---

[1] *Death and Transfiguration.*   [2] *The Banned Huntsman.*

[3] This statement, however, should be read in conjunction with a canon laid down by the same great composer when he prefixed to the most 'programmatic' of his symphonies (the *Pastoral*) the words—'Mehr Ausdruck der Empfindung als Malerey' (More expression of feeling than painting).

ON 'PROGRAMME MUSIC'

Now the forms of 'Programme Music' are necessarily often different in the main lines from those of, say, the Sonata or Symphony. A composer cannot always illustrate an historical event, or give a musical reproduction of the emotion aroused by a great picture, or by a scene of nature, and at the same time tie himself down to a form consisting of three or four set movements, nor can he always confine himself to two definite subjects stated in an 'Exposition' worked out in a 'Development', and re-stated in a 'Recapitulation'. Thus has come into existence a more fluid scheme, in which the main artistic principle of 'Unity and Variety' is observed without the adoption of a set 'form'. And thus, instead of the symphony, we often find many modern large orchestral works taking the shape of the 'Tone Poem' or 'Symphonic Poem'.

Berlioz's formal principle was the adoption of what he called an *idée fixe*, a melody representative of a person, reappearing in changed shape throughout the piece. Thus in his *Harold in Italy* he has a short theme representing the personality of Harold. Liszt employs a number of themes representing outstanding characteristics of a personality. In his *Faust* Symphony, for instance, he has themes portraying brooding inquiry, struggling aspirations, love-longing, triumphant enthusiasm, and so forth.[1] He has Faust themes and Margaret themes, and by their transformation ('transformation of themes' has become a technical term in such a connexion) he shows the play of one character on another, the gradual change of character, and so forth.

It will be evident from this that the treatment of the musical themes of a piece of modern programme music is somewhat on the general lines of that of the themes of a sonata or symphony in its 'development' portion. In fact, it is obvious that for the technical ability to shape and reshape their musical material in such a way as to reflect the ever-changing play of emotions of a Symphonic Poem the composers of to-day are indebted to the earlier composers who practised such reshaping in the Air and Variations, in the 'episodes' of the Fugue, or in the 'bridges' and 'development' of works in

[1] This, it will be seen from a later chapter, is akin to Wagner's use of the 'Leitmotiv', or leading *motif*.

Sonata form. And it follows from this that the listener who can to some extent follow the process of reshaping in these simpler and earlier forms is prepared for a fuller understanding of the more complex music of the modern forms. He who has not the power of following such processes is probably best advised to read the literary programme of a Symphonic Poem, and give himself up to any vague poetical imaginings of which his soul is capable.

It may be freely admitted that this chapter gives a by no means complete view of its subject. The same may be said of every chapter of the book, and the explanation, of course, lies in the fact that this is a book with a deliberately and carefully restricted aim—that of giving the plain man the *irreducible minimum* of knowledge necessary for the successful practice of his branch of the musical art—the Art of Listening.

4. PEACE PROCLAIMED.
Andantino. Trumpets

Treaty Signed. Amity.

V   BASS CLARINET, CLARINETS, AND BASSOONS

VI   THREE TRUMPETS

VII   THREE TROMBONES AND A TUBA

VIII   TIMPANI AND PERCUSSION

CHAPTER X

ON THE SONG, ON ORATORIO, AND ON OPERA

Music accompanied by words, or by words and action, necessarily carries with it its own explanation. The present chapter, then, will be a short one.

Song falls into two classes—(*a*) that in which a short tune, in keeping with the general idea of the poem set, is used over and over again for each verse, and (*b*) that in which the music is changed throughout the setting, adapting itself, from beginning to end, to the changing character of the words. In each case (but especially in the latter) the listener's main business is to read the poem carefully, soak himself in its thought, and give himself up to the enjoyment of its musical interpretation.

Oratorio and Opera are alike in this—each is not a 'form' but a collection of pieces in various forms. Thus there is generally an Overture (frequently in 'Sonata form', or, especially in the earlier works, embodying a piece in Fugue form). Then there are songs, and possibly short interpolated instrumental pieces, both of which may be in the 'Simple Ternary' form already described. Many of the songs are preceded by vocal declamation, in which no real 'tune' is perceptible, but in which the rhythms and inflexions of dramatic speech are imitated: this is called 'Recitative'. There are, too, choruses which may be in that same 'ternary' form, or (especially in the earlier oratorios) in Fugue form. And so forth.

In the earlier Oratorios and Operas these various divisions are pretty clearly cut off from one another. A chorus, for instance, may have no connexion (other than continuity of literary subject) with a song which precedes it. In many of the later Oratorios and Operas, however, something akin to the 'transformation of themes', explained in the last chapter, will be found, and the whole work is thus bound together as one piece. A later Opera by Wagner, or a later Oratorio by Elgar will illustrate the point very clearly.

Wagner's Music Dramas (he dropped the word 'Opera' in order to indicate his loftier artistic aims) illustrate the process clearly enough. In his great series of four dramas which go under the collective title of *The Ring of the Nibelungs*, the whole plot turns on a curse attached to a certain ring, and the ominous *motif* of the ring recurs throughout the series, as a hint of coming disaster, or as a reminder of the root-cause of some disaster just accomplished. The musical score of the whole series of dramas is woven out of a number of such *motifs*, which become in Wagner's hands a wonderfully plastic material for expression.

Similarly in Elgar's *Dream of Gerontius* we find *motifs* attached to the thought of Sleep, Fear, Judgement, and so on, and the score, again, is a beautifully woven tissue in which such *motifs* are constantly worked in, as figures in a tapestry.

In every audience at a performance of a Wagner Music Drama, or an Elgar Oratorio, there are two classes of people present who are losing a great part of the enjoyment they should obtain. The one class is made up of those who know nothing of the *motifs*, and consequently miss point after point that the composer intended them to notice. The other class is made up of conscientious, laborious souls engaged in *motif*-hunting—a sort of detective work that brings a reward of its own but from which real artistic enjoyment is almost absent. The comparatively small number of perfect listeners is made up of those who have made themselves sufficiently acquainted with the main *motifs* to recognize them subconsciously as they occur: these happy people can give themselves up to the dramatic enjoyment of the piece—and they alone get their full money's worth.

The warning as to laborious listening which brought to a close the previous chapter applies here too. If you have not enough musical knowledge to study text-books of Wagner, or annotated programmes of Elgar, to read the words of the drama or the oratorio is the best (and in your case the only) preparation. Then, steeped in the thoughts which inspired the composer, you will surely see, at least, his main drift.

CHAPTER XI

THE ORCHESTRA AND ITS INSTRUMENTS

So far as a mere layman can judge, the enjoyment of a painting depends upon three things: (1) ability to see its beauties of line or form; (2) ability to see its beauties of colouring, and (3) ability to understand its subject (where it has a subject requiring 'understanding') and, in any case, to be moved by the emotions that moved its painter as he selected his subject and did his work upon it.

In the enjoyment of a piece of orchestral music, the first two of these would appear as (1) ability to realize its beauties of melody, harmony, and 'form', and (2) ability to grasp its beauties of orchestration, whilst (3) might be expressed exactly as it was in the case of the painting.

A good deal has been said about 'form' in the earlier chapters of this book, and something about literary subject-matter (where there is a literary 'subject') in Chapter IX. It now remains to say something about the Orchestra, its instruments, and their combinations. The use of these instruments in an infinite number of different combinations gives orchestral music what is frequently spoken of as its 'colouring'. A Beethoven symphony may be likened to a glowing painting; the same symphony 'arranged' for piano solo or duet to an engraving of that painting. One may imagine that to a colour-blind person painting and engraving are of equal value, and one may say that when it comes to orchestral music, though few people, or none, are entirely colour-blind, a large number of people are partially so. Colour-blindness in music, however, is a disease that can be cured if the patient wills—and wills hard enough.

There is an anecdote about a certain Shah of Persia which gives a valuable hint or two as to the means to be adopted in the curing of this frequent partial colour-blindness. Visiting England, he was conducted on a tour of its chief sights—and sounds—and the tour included a visit to an orchestral concert. On being asked whether he had enjoyed this, he replied that there were two features of the entertainment which had impressed him favourably: he had enjoyed 'the piece that was played before the man came in and wagged the stick', and, throughout the concert, he had enjoyed watching the 'magicians who swallowed brass rods and pulled them up again'.

Now careful listening to the 'tuning-up', combined with constant observation of what the individual players of the orchestra are doing, forms the best preliminary course for any student of the art of listening who wishes to learn to appreciate orchestral colouring. The Shah, then, had made the right beginning.

Watch the players as they enter, observe the instrument each carries, see where he seats himself, note his initial movements, and then carefully store up the impression of the sounds his instrument produces in its first tentative scrapings or tootings, or blarings, or bangings. For this purpose a shilling seat on, or near, the orchestra will suit you better than a five-shilling seat in the more respectable part of the hall, and you can always migrate to the more respectable part, when, at a later concert, your preliminary survey accomplished, you are prepared to enjoy the effect of the orchestra as a whole.

See what Samuel Butler says in his *Note-book*. Accompanied by the ever-faithful Festing Jones he attended a concert of wind-instruments, and, 'I rather pleased Jones by saying that the hautbois was a clarinet with a cold in its head, and the bassoon the same with a cold in its chest'. We can be sure by this that he had been sitting near the band, and, indeed, that this was a practice with him is suggested by the opening statement of the note immediately preceding: 'We went last night to the Philharmonic and sat in the shilling orchestra, so that we could see and hear what each instrument was doing.'

Now the ability to distinguish between clarinet and oboe (Butler used the older spelling 'hautbois') is the first test in the examination for graduation as an intelligent orchestral listener. It is computed that 50 per cent. of regular attendants at orchestral concerts, and over 90 per cent. of occasional attendants, could not pass this test, were an examination chamber attached to the vestibules of our large concert halls. And were all compelled to pass through such a chamber there would be many empty seats at the concerts.

We resume our observations of the entering players, and find that they are not mere un-related individuals but members of three families—those who scrape, those who blow, and those who bang. Let us study them as families, then.

BOWED INSTRUMENTS

The 'scrapers of horsehair over cat-gut' are the most important members of the orcestra, and their leader, the chief first violin, ranks in importance after the conductor. The family has five branches—(1) the First Violins, (2) the Second Violins, (3) the Violas (or 'Altos' or 'Tenors'—variously styled), (4) the Violoncellos (Cellos for short), and (5) the Double-basses (or Contra-basses).

The **Viola** is a slightly larger Violin, and is played as such; the **Violoncello** is held between the knees as the player sits, and the **Double-bass** is so large that the player sits on a very high seat, or even stands. The First and Second Violins are identical as instruments but play different 'parts' or lines of the music. The cellos and basses, on the other hand, in the older music, and in many places in the newer also, play the same 'part', though the different pitch of the two instruments brings it about that the actual notes produced by the bass are an octave lower than those of the cello.

The pitch of these instruments naturally varies according to their size, the Violin having the highest notes and the Double-bass the lowest, but, in addition to this, the instruments vary in the quality of the tone produced. The Viola has a less brilliant but richer tone than the Violin; its tone is penetrating, and thus there are fewer Violas in the orchestra than either first or second Violins. The Cello has, again, a tone quality of its own, full and rich and very characteristic. It is impossible to describe tone in words, and that is the very reason why the reader has been advised to watch and listen as the instruments play separately: the ability to recognize the tone of an instrument is something he must acquire for himself, for no book can give it to him.

Violin, Viola, and Cello are all capable, when called on, of playing effective solo passages, whereas the Double-bass comparatively rarely has such, but is, for the most part, a mere giver of depth and strength to the bass part of the harmony.

Comparing the string family with a choir, one may say that the first and second Violins correspond to the trebles and altos, the Viola to the tenors, and the Cello to the vocal basses. The Double-bass has no counterpart in the choir, but corresponds to the organ-pedals in church, which play the bass part of a hymn-tune an octave lower than the vocal basses are singing it.

The strings are the most versatile members of the orchestra. There are so many things they can do. They can play very softly, or very loudly, they can be either bowed or plucked by the fingers ('pizzicato'), they can be 'muted' by the addition of a little clip to the bridge of the instrument, and then produce a strangely sweet, muffled tone. Further, they can either use their ordinary tones, or, the strings being very gently touched at certain points by the fingers, they can produce clear, almost 'fluty' tones, called harmonics. Very rapid passages or sustained notes are equally possible, single notes or chords can be played. The strings never need to take breath, but can continue indefinitely without rests, their tone blends with that of all other instruments or of voices, and it never palls (as does that of the other instruments). Indeed, there is hardly an end to the capabilities of the strings, and they are far and away the most expressive and valuable body of instruments in the whole orchestra.

WOOD-WIND INSTRUMENTS

The wind instruments fall into two classes—the Wood and the Brass. Let us take the Wood first.

The **Flute** is too well known to need description, but its tone should be well observed, as many people only recognize the instrument when it is playing its clear upper notes and are unaware that in its lower range it has a rich full tone of very different quality. The **Piccolo** is simply a young flute: little people make the most noise, and when the full orchestra is scraping, blowing, and banging for all it is worth, the tiny Piccolo, if it wishes, can still make its shrill high notes heard.

The normal smaller orchestra contains two Flute players, one of whom has a Piccolo handy for occasions when the score calls for its use.

The Flute, though originally made of wood, is now sometimes made of metal: it belongs, however, to the wood-wind group by its construction and by its musical characteristics.

The **Oboe** and the **Clarinet** look alike at first glance, but are very different in their construction-principles and in their tone. Both are what are called 'Reed Instruments', i.e. whereas the Flute was a simple tube, with keys added to produce the various notes, the Oboe and Clarinet have each at the mouthpiece a small detachable 'reed' or piece of thin wood; this produces the actual sound, which is then amplified, modified in tone, and controlled by means of the tube and its keys. The reed of the Oboe is a 'double reed', that of the Clarinet a 'single reed'. The tone of the Oboe is thin and piercing, though sweet; that of the Clarinet is much richer and more suave. The tone of the two instruments is much in contrast, and of this contrast composers often avail themselves. The tone of the Clarinet, by the way, varies much in its different ranges or 'registers': this should be listened for.

There is a tenor Oboe called the **Cor Anglais** (= English Horn, a misleading name, as it is no 'horn' at all), a bass Oboe called the **Bassoon,** and a double-bass Oboe called the **Contra-bassoon.** The Cor Anglais may be recognized by its resemblance to the Oboe; it is however, longer, and the mouthpiece that carries the reed is slightly bent towards the player's mouth. The Bassoon would be too long (nine feet) if its tube were extended; this is therefore bent back on itself, and the instrument takes the general shape of two tubes— a long one and a short one alongside one another. A long, gracefully-curved metal mouthpiece emerges from the upper end of the short tube. Butler's description of the tone of the Bassoon, given earlier in the chapter, though not polite nor exhaustive, will serve. The Contra-bassoon is merely the Bassoon on a larger scale.

The clarinet also exists in a bigger size—the **Bass Clarinet.** This has a curving mouthpiece (looking at first glance something like a Bassoon mouthpiece), and a metal bell at the lower end of the tube.

BRASS INSTRUMENTS

The **Horn** is a sort of 'between-maid', sometimes associating itself with the wood-wind and sometimes with its fellow brass instruments. Constructionally it belongs of course to the latter, though from the listener's point of view it must sometimes be classed with the former. It may be easily recognized if we describe it as the curly brass instrument which sometimes roars like a lion and sometimes like any sucking dove. When in the mood to do the latter it is the very poet of the orchestra. The length of its tube (Horn in F) is twelve feet—hence the curls.

The **Trumpet** most people know by sight. Its tone is also pretty well recognized. In some smaller orchestras the place of the Trumpet is taken by the Cornet, a smaller instrument of similar appearance, easier to play, but not so noble in tone.

The **Trombone** is the instrument alluded to by the Shah of the anecdote quoted earlier in this chapter. It is made in several sizes, of which the Tenor and the Bass are most commonly used to-day, the Alto having been almost discarded.

The **Bass Tuba** is the large, unwieldy brass instrument with a broad bell held upwards.

The above group of Brass instruments, ranging in pitch from the highest notes of the trumpets to the lowest of the Tuba, and in intensity from very soft to thrillingly loud, may be considered a family in themselves, capable, when called on, of playing full harmony with great effect—and with great contrast to either wood-wind or strings.

THE PERCUSSION

The **Kettledrums** or **Timpani** are copper basins having the mouth covered with parchment. They have handscrews round the rim of the basin, by which the parchment may be tightened or loosened, and by this means the pitch of the drums is raised or lowered, often during the course of a piece. From this it will be seen that the Kettledrums play fixed notes, and not the indeterminate notes of the less civilized big **Bass Drum** or of the small Drum.

There are in the orchestra at least two Kettledrums (played by one man) and the composer has these tuned to two different notes (often the first note and the fifth note of the chief key of the piece—the most important two notes in the scale): the Kettledrums then can only be used when the harmonies being played allow of the use of the notes to which they are for the moment tuned, whereas the Big Drum can come in anywhere, as a mere noise-maker.

Most people lose a lot of pleasure by never catching the softer passages of the kettledrummer; he often, at the composer's direction, plays most delicately and quite poetically, and gets little credit for it.

Used, occasionally, for a touch of red, so to speak, are the 'loud-sounding' **Cymbals** of Scripture. The **Triangle, Tambourine,** and other makers of pleasant jingle are also called on now and again. The **Glockenspiel** is a combination of metal bars, each tuned to a note and struck by hammers. The **Tubular Bells** are sufficiently described by their name: they also are tuned to notes and played by hammers.

THE HARP

One stringed instrument has received no mention above, as it did not come under the description of 'bowed instruments'. It is the **Harp:** it has no place in the orchestra of the classical symphones, but modern writers use it a great deal.

Other less frequently used instruments are briefly described in the Glossary at the end of the book.

CHAPTER XII

SOME TYPICAL ORCHESTRAL COMBINATIONS

THE HAYDN ORCHESTRA—LATER EIGHTEENTH CENTURY

The tendency in orchestral writing is consistently towards larger combinations. New instruments are introduced, and larger numbers of the old ones called for. Here is the classical orchestra of the days of Haydn, the 'Father of the Symphony', as used in his *Paukenwirbel* (= Drum Roll) *Symphony*—so called because it begins with a roll on the Kettledrum.

Wood-wind (8 players).
    2 Flutes
    2 Oboes
    2 Clarinets
    2 Bassoons

Brass (4 players).
    2 Horns
    2 Trumpets

Percussion (1 player).
    2 Kettledrums

Strings.
    1st and 2nd Violins, Violas, 'Cellos, and Double basses.

THE BEETHOVEN ORCHESTRA—EARLY NINETEENTH CENTURY

The various scores of any composer differ in the instruments they call for, but a typical work of the composer gives us his average demands. Let us take the famous Fifth Symphony.

SOME TYPICAL ORCHESTRAL COMBINATIONS

Wood-wind (10 players).
- 2 Flutes + 1 Piccolo (i.e. 3 players)
- 2 Oboes
- 2 Clarinets
- 2 Bassoons
- 1 Double-bassoon

Brass (7 players).
- 2 Horns
- 2 Trumpets
- 3 Trombones (Alto, Tenor, and Bass)

Percussion (1 player).
- 2 Kettledrums

Strings.
As in the case of Haydn (but Beethoven would have a larger number of players to each 'part').

THE ELGAR ORCHESTRA—EARLY TWENTIETH CENTURY

Let us examine the score of Elgar's Second Symphony (see pp. 70, 71). Note that by this date we have complete groups of Flutes (3), of Oboes (2 Oboes + Cor Anglais + 2 Bassoons + Double-bassoon), of Clarinets (1 E flat—a high-pitched instrument commonly used in military bands; 2 normal Clarinets, and 1 Bass Clarinet), of Horns (4), of Trumpets (3), and so forth.

Wood-wind (13 players).
- 3 Flutes (one of whom plays also Piccolo)
- 2 Oboes
- 1 Cor Anglais
- 1 Clarinet in E flat
- 2 Clarinets in B flat
- 1 Bass Clarinet
- 2 Bassoons
- 1 Double-bassoon

Brass (11 players).
- 4 Horns
- 3 Trumpets
- 3 Trombones
- 1 Tuba

Percussion (3 players).
- 3 Kettledrums: one player
- 1 Side Drum and 1 Tambourine (one player)
- 1 Big Drum and Cymbals (one player)

Plucked Strings (2 players).
- 2 Harps

Bowed Strings.

As in the Beethoven score, but Elgar not infrequently divides his first violins, his second violins, his violas and 'cellos into two parts each, making (with the double-basses) nine string parts. Obviously to do this, and also to balance the greatly increased wind department, he needs a very much larger body of stringed-instrument players than was actually required by Beethoven.

SOME HINTS ON LISTENING

In learning to listen to an orchestra, note passages played by strings alone, by wood-wind alone, and by brass alone, and get the effect well into your mind. Then notice passages where individual instruments are used in contrast to one another, as, for instance, where a snatch of melody is given to Flute, to Oboe, and to Clarinet in turn. Try, in short, to hear what is being done and to notice who is doing it. At first use your eyes to help your ears. In time (and perhaps more quickly than you imagine) you will gain the power of hearing a great deal that you formerly missed, and your enjoyment will be enhanced proportionately.

In the early stages it will help you more to hear Haydn than Beethoven, and Beethoven than Strauss or Elgar. Indeed, a seaside pier, with its small band, may be a more useful laboratory for your researches than the great concert halls of London or New York, with their bands of three or four times as many players. The Cornet and Flute you can sometimes study in the street; Clarinet tone you can study whenever a military band is playing (the Clarinets are the strings of the military band). Be on the watch for opportunities of hearing the instruments in isolation, so that you may learn later to recognize them in combination.

CHAPTER XIII

THE CHAIN OF COMPOSERS

What we *expect* has a good deal to do with what we *hear*—as already hinted somewhere in this book. As has been said, the man who goes to hear a Symphony not knowing what a Symphony is often gets lost during the first five minutes. And the man who goes to hear Bach not knowing who Bach was, and what sort of music he wrote, is likely to be just as quickly bewildered and just as greatly disappointed.

One can, indeed, imagine a man who had been brought up on Beethoven and post-Beethoven, and who had heard nothing of earlier date, indignantly demanding his money back after a Bach concert. Similarly, one can imagine a man who had been brought up on Bach and his contemporaries and predecessors scornfully turning on his heels after the first fifteen minutes of a concert of Beethoven. And, further, very easily one can picture a violent riot amongst an audience brought up on both Bach and Beethoven and suddenly introduced to some work of Stravinsky.[1]

For the most part these troubles would arise through wrong expectations. It is conceivable that Bach, Beethoven, and Stravinsky are pretty nearly equally 'great'. Admit, for the sake of argument, that they *are* equally 'great', and it is nevertheless true that it is useless to listen to Bach with the Beethoven mind, to Beethoven with the Bach mind, or to Stravinsky with either of those minds. Competent listening demands the historical sense: there is hardly such a thing as 'absolute' listening, it is always 'relative'. Composers themselves hardly understand this. Stravinsky told the present writer that Bach and Beethoven made hardly any appeal to him, and other composers have made similar confessions. Often the greatest com-

[1] Such riots, in fact, once nearly occurred in London.

posers have been unable to appreciate even their own contemporaries where those worked with different aims, and expressed different national or individual minds.

Art is very various, and it is probably useless for anyone to try to appreciate it in all its manifestations, but the worst form of narrowness, at any rate, may be avoided, and even a little historical and biographical study helps surprisingly. As already stated in an earlier chapter, study of this kind involves the reading of special works, the present book being concerned chiefly with the structural side of music. One or two such works are mentioned in an appendix, but a very brief survey of the field is perhaps worth while here. It necessarily follows conventional lines.

THE EARLY CONTRAPUNTAL WRITERS—SIXTEENTH CENTURY

Although there is now more interest in earlier times, music heard in our concert-rooms, theatres, and churches dates from the sixteenth century or later. The best work of that century is the culmination of the earlier contrapuntal school. Such composers as the British BYRD or the Italian PALESTRINA may be taken as representative. Their works are 'woven' rather than built, i.e. strands of melody are twisted in and out amongst one another. This conception must already be familiar enough to readers, from the earlier chapters. The work of Byrd, Palestrina, and other contemporaries followed on two or three centuries of experiment in the development of contrapuntal processes, and with this work music attained its first climax.

Much of the work of this period is written not in our modern scales, but in certain old scales called **Modes.** The Choral Music of the day (Church Music, such as Masses, and Home Music, such as Madrigals) is invariably intended for unaccompanied singing.

Keyboard Music was first developed at this period, and the men who developed it were that brilliant group of English players and composers whose centre was the London of Queen Elizabeth and James I: these were the men who discovered what types of passage-work really suited fingers on the keyboard, and began to observe what forms were really fitted for instrumental music.

SYMPHONY No. 2.
In E flat.
I.

Edward Elgar, Op. 63.

Copyright, 1911, by Novello and Company, Limited

Printed by F.M.Geidel, Leipzig

THE EARLY HARMONIC SCHOOL—SEVENTEENTH CENTURY

Then in the early seventeeth century came a new view. **Opera** and **Oratorio** were devised by Italian composers, and the basis of their early experiments was that imitation of speech in song already mentioned in an early chapter under the name of **Recitative** (p. 55). Instrumental accompaniment to this recitative took the form of simple chords, merely supporting the voice at suitable points, and thus attention was drawn to chords as such, and the **harmonic aspect** of music began to attract composers.

A great deal of contrapuntal music was written, as it always has been, and probably always will be. But the balance began to fall on the side of harmony rather than counterpoint. Putting it crudely—in the sixteenth century composers wove melodies together and chords resulted: in the seventeenth century they devised successions of chords, and, with these as a basis, worked out combinations of melodies.

The old modes began to disappear and the modern scales to become universal. It was the study of harmonic possibilities that caused this. In effect composers discarded those of the modes apparently least suitable for varied harmonic effects, and retained the two most suitable for such. Unaccompanied choral singing of any serious kind died out.

THE LATER CONTRAPUNTAL SCHOOL—EARLY EIGHTEENTH CENTURY

Thoroughly understanding now both Harmony and Counterpoint, composers like Purcell were able to bring music gradually to the second of its climactic points. BACH and HANDEL represent the actual climax. Bach wrote the finest instrumental Fugues ever written, and a great deal of other fine Keyboard Music. He also wrote incredible quantities of Church Music—Cantatas, settings of the Passion, a wonderful Mass, &c. Handel wrote Keyboard Music, too, and a great many Oratorios and Operas. The general basis of the work of both is Counterpoint—but Counterpoint devised with great Harmonic mastery.

Up to this point the Orchestra had not been standardized, i.e. its constituent instruments varied greatly on different occasions. Also the effective way of writing for orchestra—the tossing about of a little phrase from one instrument to another, and the constant alternation of different tone-colour combinations—had not been discovered. (Many music listeners have never realized the existence of a constant element of 'discovery' or 'invention' in the progress of music.)

THE SONATA AND SYMPHONY PERIOD—LATER EIGHTEENTH CENTURY

Bach and Handel were the last great names in the Contrapuntal-Harmonic School. They carried their style as far as it could go, and a new beginning had to be made. Whilst they were finishing their life-work a group of younger composers (including one of Bach's sons) were making a new beginning. The modern piano and the modern orchestra were now coming into being, and the new development was largely an instrumental one: it brought into existence the modern **Sonata** and **Symphony** (already fully explained in earlier chapters), and the great names of the period are HAYDN and MOZART. The sonata-symphony plan became a recognized formula, and works on that plan became the staple of orchestral or keyboard performance. The period was one of great perfecting of Form: often, too, a good deal of feeling was infused into the music, but it is a convenient generalization to call this period one of the development of formal beauty in music, rather than of emotional expression.

Modern Orchestration now came into being.

THE EARLIER ROMANTIC PERIOD—EARLY NINETEENTH CENTURY

Now came BEETHOVEN, who sat at the feet of Haydn and Mozart, learnt all they had to teach about the sonata-symphony form, and then, using that form as the instrument of his more passionate nature, expressed by its means deeper feelings than they had dreamt capable of musical expression. He took their mould and poured his thoughts into it red-hot: perhaps sometimes the mould cracked a

74 THE CHAIN OF COMPOSERS

bit here and there under the process, but still he used the mould His work marks modern music's third climax.

It is convenient to apply the word 'Classical' to music of the Bach-Handel period, and the word 'Romantic' to the period that begins with Beethoven, associating with him SCHUBERT and WEBER. The terms 'Classical' and 'Romantic' are, however, very slippery terms to handle. It would be possible to speak of Bach and Handel as 'Classical', and of Mozart and Haydn as the founders of the Romantic School. And some people go to the other extreme and call Beethoven Classical, beginning the Romantic School with Schumann. The fact is that there are Romantic elements everywhere—in Purcell and Bach even. Music being an Art, not a Science, exact terminology is difficult or impossible; all one can hope to do is to convey some fairly sound general ideas, and to trust a good deal to the common sense of readers not to take one too literally.

The development of orchestral writing during this period has already been made evident in the chapters upon the Orchestral Combinations.

THE MIDDLE ROMANTIC PERIOD

MENDELSSOHN, SCHUMANN, and CHOPIN are the outstanding names of this period, and, of these three, Schumann most completely represents it. In his works one sees the intrusion of a large literary element, and he is the romantic of the romantics. The expression of national feeling in music now becomes common, and the Polish-French Chopin may be taken as a handy example of this. The piano is now thoroughly domesticated, and small piano pieces become a more popular medium of expression than the Sonata.

THE LATER ROMANTICS—MIDDLE OF NINETEENTH CENTURY

BERLIOZ, LISZT, WAGNER, VERDI, and BRAHMS represent this period. As something has been said about Berlioz and Liszt under the heading of 'Programme Music', their work may be left unexplained here, except that it may be added that Berlioz greatly developed orchestral resources, and Liszt piano virtuosity.

As for Wagner, more must be added, but before this can be done we must retrace our steps a little and summarize the development of Opera. The invention of this form has been alluded to. In its early stages it was essentially dramatic, its dependence on Recitative (an actual imitation of speech) indicating its realistic aim. Soon it became more formal, and the development of the Aria (a song form on a strict I–II–I plan) indicates this clearly enough, for how can the hero and heroine be intensely dramatic when their songs are so definitely cut and dried in their shape, and when the action of the stage has to cease whilst they are singing each? A mass of other conventions also grew up around Opera, and the first sturdy attempt to disperse them was made by Gluck in the eighteenth century. Then Weber came along and brought the more obvious romanticism into Opera, with a great deal of German national feeling. Wagner carried the Gluck and Weber propaganda further. He aimed not at a string of Recitatives and Arias, but at a real dramatic whole, which after his first works he began to call **Music Drama** (see p. 56). This he intended should be a reasonable combination of all the arts, no concessions being made to music as such. How far he succeeded in this main aim and how far he failed is matter for discussion in larger books than this.

Wagner chose intensely national German subjects. He developed the orchestra immensely, he almost abandoned set airs, and adopted instead a sort of Recitative which rose to a more continuously melodic style at the moments of high emotion, and he wove together his very contrapuntal orchestral score out of a mass of *motifs*, each associated with some personality, quality, or phase of thought. (This, however, has been alluded to earlier, p. 56.)

In a class of his own was the Italian opera composer Verdi, a great national figure whose life spanned almost the entire nineteenth century. He had in full measure the characteristic Italian understanding of the human voice, and both vocally and dramatically his works represent a peak of operatic achievement only equalled in that century by that of Wagner.

Brahms may be styled a classical-romantic. 'He was neither a pioneer nor a revolutionary; he was, like Bach, merely the most mighty wielder of the forces which his time had inherited.'[1] He wrote no operas, but stands for high aim and achievement in piano music, orchestral music, chamber music, songs, and choral music.

The nationalistic Russians—Glinka, Mussorgsky, Borodin, Rimsky-Korsakof—did much wonderful work which had to wait far too long for its general European popularity.

THE TURN OF THE CENTURY

It is convenient to class under this heading DVOŘÁK, FRANCK, GRIEG, TCHAIKOVSKY, STRAUSS, WOLF, DEBUSSY, RAVEL, ELGAR, DELIUS, SIBELIUS, ALBENIZ, GRANADOS, TURINA, FALLA, CASELLA, PIZZETTI, RESPIGHI, and PUCCINI. Dvořák was a Bohemian nationalist composer; Franck was a Belgian-French Catholic mystic, influenced by Bach and Beethoven; Grieg a nationalist Norwegian composer; Tchaikovsky a Russian orchestral composer, not very national in his musical idiom, but with the excitability (and sometimes morbidity) of his countrymen. Strauss was the outstanding German composer of the period: his operas and tone poems combine a technical wizardry with an opulence of style which strongly appeals to some tastes, and is over-rich for others. Wolf was an Austrian composer of many fine songs; Debussy was an impressionist Frenchman with a very delicate style. Ravel was a Frenchman who contributed much to the subtleties of the musical language; his music has, at first hearing, a certain likeness to that of Debussy. Elgar was one of the greatest British composers since Purcell. His work was divided about equally between oratorio and orchestral composition. Delius wrote fine choral and orchestral music and several operas. Sibelius was a strongly nationalist Finnish composer who left seven great symphonies of marked originality. Albeniz, Granados, Turina, and Falla represent the strongly national modern Spanish School. Casella, Pizzetti, and Respighi in Italy showed a progressive outlook, in some contrast with the rather superficial Italian operatic fashion. The impact of the operas of Puccini, however, one of the most popular of all operatic composers, is not to be belittled.

[1] Colles, *The Growth of Music.*

TODAY

The greatest figures of our own time, STRAVINSKY, BARTÓK, SCHOENBERG and VAUGHAN WILLIAMS, were all born between 1872 and 1882. They are our link with the nineteenth century, but they were adventurous, forward-looking composers. Both Bartók, the leading Hungarian composer, and Vaughan Williams were deeply affected by the folk music of their respective countries, which in turn influenced their own compositions. Stravinsky also started off as a strongly nationalistic composer, and his early, obviously Russian-flavoured works are still justly popular. But perhaps because he was successively a citizen of four different countries (Russia, Switzerland, France, and the United States of America), Stravinsky shed much of the Russian influence. His style has undergone as many transformations as has the painting of his contemporary Picasso: like Picasso too, Stravinsky remained a lively and controversial figure throughout his long career.

Schoenberg, the Austrian composer, forged for himself an almost new language of composition which still sounds strange to many of us but with the passage of years is becoming less so, and has been a great influence on many younger composers of all countries. Two other Austrian composers, just junior to Schoenberg and pupils of his, are also key figures of the period: ALBAN BERG, known chiefly by his powerful, if neurotic, opera *Wozzeck*, and ANTON VON WEBERN. Standing outside this Austrian school of advanced, often problematical music is the much more traditional, but entirely modern-sounding, German composer HINDEMITH.

English music of the present century has certainly held its own in comparison with the music of continental Europe. VAUGHAN WILLIAMS, already mentioned, left us a wonderful and varied series of nine symphonies, and some of the finest choral music of our time. HOLST, his contemporary and close friend, still perhaps under-rated, was a pioneer in his time: one work of his at least, *The Planets*, is in the international orchestral repertoire. Of the English composers who have followed, WALTON and BRITTEN, the former especially in the orchestral field and the latter with his operas, have gained a world-wide reputation.

Of the other great countries of the world, Russia has produced two major composers in PROKOFIEV and SHOSTAKOVICH, while the United States of America has, in IVES and COPLAND, at least two composers of like status. Moreover, the USA is making a vital contribution to music in the theatre, both light and serious.

It is necessary, perhaps, to warn the reader that nothing in this chapter is true! How can one generalize in so rough and ready a way and yet be accurate? At the most one can convey a vague idea and leave the readers to find their own means of correcting this and filling it out by the thoughtful perusal of some larger book. And, of course, the contents of this chapter need to be read in conjunction with those of the previous chapters. What is said in the chapter on Programme Music, for instance, has to be remembered in reading what is written here about 'The Later Romantics' and about 'To-day'.

We have tried, perhaps very rashly, to compress into a few pages a sketch of the development of music during a period of four hundred years or so. The title we have chosen speaks of the succession of composers as a chain, and it may be emphasized that this description is a true one. Every composer of merit is a *link*, depending from some link above him and suspending some link below. Consider, for instance, the growth of the modern sonata and symphony form. Though it has been called above a new beginning, and though this in a sense is true, yet on close examination it will be found that the form developed out of the eighteenth-century Suite. There is here a series of links then—the great Sebastian Bach, his son Emanuel Bach, Haydn, Mozart, Beethoven, and so on. Wagner did not write symphonies,[1] but for his whole development he was greatly indebted to the influence of Beethoven. Even when a composer seems so individual as to stand alone a close study of his works in the order of their composition will show them to be founded upon the works of some earlier composer.

---

[1] A youthful symphony in C major exists but composition in the symphonic form was no part of Wagner's life-work.

Brief as this chapter may be it will yet serve to show the growing scope in music, which is all the time striving to learn how to express more and more of the spirit of man. The study of how it does this is infinite in its possible extent, and to anyone undertaking it may be recommended two main lines of research—the expression of *personality* and the expression of *nationality* in music.

APPENDIX

BOOKS FOR ADDITIONAL READING

History and Biography. Scholes, *The Listener's History of Music; A Miniature History of Music* (Oxford University Press); Mellers (ed.), *Man and His Music* (Barrie and Jenkins); Stevens (ed.), *The Pelican History of Music* (Pelican); the *Master Musicians* series (Dent), consisting of a large number of separate volumes, each devoted to one composer.

Form. Abraham, *Design in Music* (Oxford University Press); Cooke, *The Language of Music* (Oxford University Press); Macpherson, *Music and its Appreciation* (Joseph Williams); Morris, *The Structure of Music* (Oxford University Press); Tobin, *How to Understand Musical Form* (Boosey & Hawkes).

Orchestra. Borland, *The Instruments of the Orchestra* (H. W. Gray Co. and Novello); Fiske, *Score Reading:* Bk. I, *Orchestration*, Bk. II, *Musical Form*, Bk. III, *Concertos*, Bk. IV, *Oratorios* (Oxford University Press); Howes, *The Fontana Guide to Orchestral Music* (Collins); Mason, *The Orchestral Instruments and what they do: a Primer for Concert-goers* (H. W. Gray & Co. and Novello); Montagu-Nathan, *The Orchestra and How to Listen to it* (Kegan Paul).

All the above are *simple* books. There is no end to the more difficult books on such subjects, and the *Oxford Companion to Music* and Grove's *Dictionary of Music and Musicians* may be consulted on specific points. The latter has bibliographies at the end of each entry.

CONCERT-GOER'S GLOSSARY

OF TERMS FOUND IN PROGRAMMES

The professional or skilled amateur musician does not in the least realize the puzzling appearance an ordinary concert programme presents to a musically unlearned concert-goer. Such a programme is literally bespattered with highly technical terms in four languages. Hence it has been thought well to provide this book with a Glossary including a brief explanation of musical terms found in programmes.

The complete Glossary is not, of course, a 'Dictionary of Musical Terms', but it is probable that it contains most of the words required by the concert-goer without musical training for whom this book is written. It would be worth the while of such a reader to go straight through this Glossary as a completion of his study of this book. Where he finds a reference to earlier pages let him search his memory as to the knowledge he has gained of the point in question, and then turn up the reference as a test of his correct re-collection of it. Where, on the other hand, he finds new information that strikes him as useful, let him make a mental note of it.

ABBREVIATIONS

Fr. = French. It. = Italian. Ger. = German.

Accelerando (It.). Getting quicker and quicker.
Accent. See p. 4.
Acciaccatura (It.). A short *Appoggiatura* (q.v.).
Adagio (It.). Slow. Often used as a name for the slow 'movement' of a sonata or similar work.
Ad libitum. At will.
Affrettato (It.) and similar words, all parts of the Italian verb *affrettare*, to hasten.
Agitato (It.). Agitated.
Agité (Fr.). Agitated.

Air de Ballet (Fr.). A ballet tune. (See **Ballet**.)
Air with Variations. See pp. 26, 37, 38, 42-3, 53, 60.
Albumblatt (Ger.). Literally 'Album-leaf'; hence a short instrumental piece of lighter character.
Alcuno (It.). Some; e.g. *Con alcuna licenza*, with some freedom.
Alla breve (It.). With a minim to each beat. The minim, despite its name, is a fairly long note, and the idea is that, whereas a minim usually has two beats, when this

indication occurs it is to have only one. Hence the pace is to be quicker than might be supposed.

Allargando (It.). Getting gradually slower and broader.

Allegrezza (It.). Joyfulness.

Allegro (It.). Lively and bright. Often used as the title of a piece or movement of this character.

Allegretto (It.). Rather lively and bright (diminutive of *Allegro*). Often used as the title of a piece or movement of this character.

Allemande (Fr.). A piece in dance rhythm, in four-beat time and of lively character. It found a place in the seventeenth and eighteenth century suites, generally as the opening movement.

Althorn, or Tenor or Baritone, a sort of saxhorn (q.v.).

Alto. (*a*) The second voice of an ordinary male voice church choir, i.e. below the treble and above the tenor; it is the highest adult male voice, and is really a falsetto.

(*b*) In instrumental music Alto usually means the viola (also called Tenor. See p. 59).

Amore (It.). Love, e.g. *Con amore.*

Andante (It.). Literally 'going', i.e. neither fast nor slow. Often used as the title for a piece or movement in this style.

Andantino (It.). At a gently moving pace. Often used as the title for a piece or movement in this style.

Animando (It.). Gradually becoming animated.

Animato (It.). Animated.

Animé (Fr.). Animated.

'Answer' in fugue. See p. 43.

Aperto (It.). Lit. 'open', i.e. distinct, clear.

Appassionato (It.). With passion. (Beethoven has a *Sonata Appassionata*—so called not by him but by one of his publishers.)

Appoggiatura (It.). A little 'grace note', prefixed to the principal note. It is generally the note immediately below or above the latter.

Arabesque. An ornamental figure in melody (the equivalent in music of the arabesque in linear design or architecture, see p. 26). Or a piece employing melodic figures of this character.

Aria (It.). An air or song, generally on somewhat extended scale and in form as follows: first part, second part, first part repeated. The songs in eighteenth-century operas and oratorios were generally in this form See **Da Capo**, also p. 75.

Arpeggio (It.). A chord spread out in playing, harp fashion.

Arrangement. Generally the same as *Transcription* (q.v.)

Assai (It.). Enough, i.e. very.

Assez (Fr.). Enough, i.e. fairly.

Aubade (Fr.). A morning song (cf. *Serenade*, an evening song).

Augmentation. Making longer the notes of a 'subject' or musical theme. For instance, a fugue subject which appeared originally in short notes may be given later in longer notes. The reverse process of *Diminution* may also occur.

Badinerie (Fr.). A playful bantering piece.

Bagatelle (Fr. or Ger.) (plural in Ger. **Bagatellen**). A trifle, a short piece of instrumental music. Beethoven and others have used the term.

Bagpipe. A well-known instrument once popular all over Europe and still played in Scotland, Brittany, and elsewhere. A bag serves as a receptacle for the air blown into it by the player. One or more pipes produce unvarying *Drone Notes* and a *Chanter* pipe, played by the fingers, supplies the tune.

Ballade (Fr.). In piano music a piece rather fancifully intended to embody the idea of narrative, e.g. the Ballades of Chopin.

Ballata (It.). A short song, or an

instrumental piece in song style, and generally in a dance rhythm.

Ballet. A piece intended for stage dancing. The old-fashioned operas had irrelevant decorative ballets introduced. Nowadays the ballet tends to become a form of art in its own right, expressive and dramatic rather than merely decorative.

Bar (=Measure). The notes of a piece are grouped in sets called bars or measures, each set being of equal time value, i.e. each bar having two beats, three beats, four beats, &c. in it, according to the time signature at the beginning of the piece. See p. 5. The word 'Bar' is also applied to the lines drawn through the score which mark off from one another the bars (in the above sense), i.e. the measures.

Barcarolle (Fr.). A boat song, or, in instrumental music, an imitation of such, with a rowing rhythm.

Baritone. (a) A voice, in pitch between bass and tenor. (b) Another name for the althorn, a sort of saxhorn. See **Saxhorn**.

Bass. (a) The lowest voice of the normal choir. (b) The lowest part of the harmony. (c) The lowest instrument of a combination.

Bass Drum. The Big Drum. See p. 62.

Basset Horn (= Corno di Bassetto). As the cor anglais is to the oboe so is the basset horn to the clarinet, i.e. each may be considered the alto of its kind (despite their names neither is a horn in any sense). The basset horn is now rarely used.

Bass Flute. A flute now obsolete.

Bassoon. See p. 61.

Bass Tuba. See p. 62; also under **Saxhorn**.

Beat (or Pulse). See p. 4.

Bells (Tubular Bells). See p. 63.

Binary. See p. 28.

Bolero (much the same as *Cachucha*). A Spanish dance with three beats in the bar and castanets accompaniment.

Bourrée. A dance form in four-beat rhythm, often used as one of the movements in the old suites.

Bowed Instruments. See p. 59.

Brass. See p. 62.

Bravura (It.). Brilliance in execution.

Breve. The longest note used in music, the equal in value of two semibreves.

Bridge Passages. See Ch. VI and subsequent chapters.

Brio (It.). Spirit, e.g. *Con brio*.

Broken Chord. A chord played in the fashion of an *Arpeggio* (q.v.), instead of with all of its notes together.

Cachucha. Much the same as *Bolero* (q.v.).

Cadence (or **Close**). A point of rest in a piece, such as the two chords which bring the whole piece to an end; or of rest and new beginning, such as the two chords which end a phrase or sentence (see p. 4) and hint at another phrase or sentence to follow. Cadences are therefore the 'punctuation' of music. The *Perfect Cadence* (or *Full Close*) which ends a piece, or section of a piece, corresponds to a full stop; it consists of the chord of the dominant followed by the chord of the tonic. The *Imperfect Cadence* (or *Half Close*) may be considered a comma; it consists of some chord followed by the chord of the dominant. The *Interrupted Cadence* leads one to think that a perfect cadence is coming and then gently shocks one by showing that it is not; it generally consists of the dominant chord followed by the sub-mediant chord, and corresponds perhaps to the dash in punctuation. The *Plagal Cadence* is often used as a final 'clincher', after the perfect cadence, and is familiar as the most frequent 'Amen' after a hymn; it consists of the subdominant chord followed by the tonic chord.

Cadenza (It.). (*a*) A passage of mere vocal display, introduced by old composers as a concession to the vanity of the singer. (*b*) A similar instrumental passage in a concerto, designed to allow the solo performer to show off. Formerly a mere blank space (so to speak) was left for him by the composer in his score, near the end of a movement. The orchestra then sat silent for a space, and the soloist was left to fill in as he liked. Nowadays composers are more wary, and write out in full what they want the performer to play. Thus they are able to make the cadenza a real part of the piece, instead of a mere excrescence, as it often tended to become in the past.

Calando (It.). Gradually dying away in tone, and getting slower and slower at the same time.

Canon. A contrapuntal piece in which two or more parts or voices exactly imitate one another—*Three Blind Mice* style.

Cantabile (It.). In a singing style.

Cantando (It.) = *Cantabile* (q.v.).

Cantata. Formerly an extended piece for solo voice, now generally a small oratorio or secular work of similar style.

Cantilena (It.). (*a*) A short song. (*b*) In a singing style.

Canto (It.). Song, or an instrumental piece in song style, e.g. *Canto d'amore* = a love song.

Canto fermo (It.). A 'fixed song', i.e. a piece of melody around which other melodies are woven contrapuntally.

Capellmeister (Ger.). A conductor (in Germany) holding some permanent post. The term has acquired a sinister meaning in 'Capellmeister Music', i.e. academic stuff, such as any trained musician can construct according to rule.

Cappella, A cappella (It.). 'In the church style', i.e. the sixteenth-century church style hence *unaccompanied* choral music (this is the most common use of the term).

Capriccio (It.) = *Caprice* (q.v.).

Caprice. A short piece of instrumental music of the style suggested by the word.

Castanets or **Castagnets.** An instrument of Spanish origin consisting of two small pieces of wood to be clicked together. Used as an accompaniment to some Spanish dances. See **Bolero** and **Fandango.**

Cavatina (It.). A short simple song, or instrumental piece in that style.

Celesta. A percussion instrument, consisting of metal plates struck by hammers played from a keyboard.

Cello or **Violoncello.** See pp. 59, 60.

Cembalo (It.). A shortened form of a name for the harpsichord, *Clavicembalo*. The word will be found in old scores of the Bach-Handel period, when the harpsichord was a member of the orchestra. See **Figured Bass** and **Harpsichord.**

Chaconne (Fr.) or **Ciacona** (It.). A dance form in rather slow time, generally on a Ground Bass (q.v.).

Chalumeau. The lowest portion of the compass (i.e. lowest 'register') of the clarinet. It has a characteristic tone quality, different from that of the upper registers.

Chamber Music. An arbitrary term. It ought to mean such music as can be performed in a room in distinction from such as requires concert-hall, church, or theatre, but actually it means concerted music for two, three, four, five, six, seven, eight, or nine instruments, e.g. the string trio, quartet, &c.

Chanter. See **Bagpipe.**

Choral (or **Chorale**). A Lutheran hymn-tune. Bach used such tunes greatly as a basis for his instrumental and choral works, e.g. his organ choral preludes, in which some choral is used as the chief thematic material.

Chord. See p. 6.

Chords of 6th (or $^6_3$ and $^6_4$). The most ordinary chord is made up of a note and its 3rd and 5th (e.g. C, E, G). Invert this (so that E is the bass note) and we get a chord of the 3rd and 6th (called a six-three chord, or a chord of the 6th). Invert again (so that G is the bass) and we get a chord of the 4th and 6th (called a six-four chord).

Chromatic. Proceeding by semitones, as for instance the 'chromatic scale'. A chromatic chord is one in which one or more notes have been raised or lowered a semitone by the use of sharps or flats, i.e. one containing a note or notes outside the diatonic scale of the key the music is in at the time.

Chromatic Drums. A variety of kettledrums or timpani, which can be re-tuned quickly to any desired note by means of a single screw.

Chromatic Scale. See **Scale.**

Chromatic Semitone. A semitone such as that from a note to its own sharp or flat. C to C sharp is a *Chromatic Semitone.* B to C a *Diatonic Semitone.*

Church Modes. See **Modes.**

Ciacona = *Chaconne* (q.v.).

Clarinet. See pp. 58, 61.

Classical. A term of doubtful and varying meaning, explained on p. 74. *Classical* as distinguished from *Popular*, p. 7.

Clavier. A Keyboard.

Close. See **Cadence.**

Coda (It.). See pp. 24-26, 31-33, 36-38.

Codetta (It.). A small Coda.

Col legno (It.). Lit. 'with the wood', i.e. (in violin playing) using the back of the bow to strike the strings.

Colouring. See pp. 9, 57, and **Tone Colour.**

Come (It.). As, or Like, e.g. *Come Prima* = as at first.

Commodo or **Comodo** (It.). 'Convenient', e.g. *Tempo comodo* = at a convenient speed.

Common Chord. A chord consisting of a bass note and the 3rd and perfect 5th above it. (Sometimes called a $^5_3$ chord.) See also **Interval.**

Compound Time. Time in which each beat is divisible into three smaller beats. See **Bar.**

Con (It.). With, e.g. *Con moto*, with motion, speed.

Concert Overture. See **Overture.**

Concertante (*adj.*) (It.). (*a*) Used of several solo instruments or voices performing together. (*b*) Suitable for concert use.

Concertino (It.). (*a*) A small Concerto. (*b*) A principal player, as distinguished from *Ripieno* (q.v.).

Concerto (It.). See p. 35.

Concertstück (Ger.). Lit. 'Concerted piece', a description applied to a continuous piece for one chief instrument (or more) and orchestra, not a full-blown Concerto with several movements. Or, simply, a 'concert-piece'.

Consort of Instruments. An old-fashioned term for any small combination of instruments.

Contrabass or **Double-Bass.** See pp. 59, 60.

Contrabass Clarinet. An instrument an octave lower than the *Bass Clarinet*; sometimes called *Pedal Clarinet* (though the feet have nothing to do with it).

Contrafagotto (It.) or **Double Bassoon.** See p. 61.

Contralto. See **Alto.** As regards pitch, the contralto voice is the feminine equivalent of the masculine alto, and in choral music if altos and contraltos are both present they sing the same 'part'. The alto is, however, the highest adult male voice and the contralto the lowest female voice.

Contrapuntal. See p. 6.

Cor Anglais (Fr.) or **Corno Inglese** (It.). See p. 61.

Cornet. See p. 62.

Corno di Bassetto (It.) = *Basset Horn* (q.v.).

'Counter-Answer' in fugue. See p. 45.

Counter-Motive. A *Motif* (see p. 30) written to be performed at the same time as another one.

Counterpoint. See pp. 6, 8, 42.

'Counter-Subject' in fugue. See p. 45.

Courante (Fr.). A dance piece in three-beat time, found as a constituent member of the eighteenth-century suite.

Crescendo (It.). Getting gradually louder.

Crotchet. One of the shorter notes in music, equal in value to half a minim or to two quavers.

Cyclic Forms. Forms consisting of several 'movements' (see p. 36), as the sonata, symphony, suite, the classical String Quartet, &c.

Cymbals. Plates of brass clanged by the player of the big drum or his assistant. See p. 63.

Da Capo (It.). From the beginning, i.e. go back and repeat the first part of the piece. Often abbreviated D.C. The term was often used in the eighteenth-century aria (q.v.).

Deciso (It.). With a decided feeling for the beat.

Demisemiquaver. One of the shortest notes in music, half a semiquaver.

Descant. See *Discant*.

Desiderio (It.). Desire, e.g. *Con desiderio*, with yearning.

Development. Ch. VI and subsequent chapters.

Diatonic. According to the notes of the ordinary major or minor scale, as distinguished from the chromatic (q.v.).

Diatonic Scale. See **Scale.**

Diatonic Semitone. See **Chromatic Semitone.**

Diminuendo (It.). Getting gradually softer in tone.

Diminution. Making shorter the notes of a 'subject' or musical theme. For instance, a fugue subject which appeared originally in long notes may be given later in short notes. The reverse process is called 'augmentation'.

Discant (or **Descant**). An early form of counterpoint; an added part woven in with an existing part.

Discord. See **Dissonance.**

Dissonance. A combination of notes which sounds harsh, or at least is unsatisfactory *in itself* and requires following in some particular way in order to become acceptable to the ear, i.e. requires 'Resolution'.

Divertimento (It.). A light and lively piece.

Divisi (It.). Divided. Used of strings in orchestra, e.g. of first violins, when instead of these all playing the same they are divided into two or more parts. See p. 66.

Dolce (It.). Sweet. The superlative *Dolcissimo* is also used.

Dolente (It.). Sorrowful.

Dolore (It.). Pain, sadness.

Dominant. The fifth note of the scale, and the next most important to the tonic.

Dominant Seventh. A very frequent chord in music, consisting of the dominant, with its third, fifth, and seventh (e.g. in the key of C, the notes are G, B, D, F).

Double = *a Variation* (see p. 27), e.g. *Air with Doubles* (a sixteenth or seventeenth-century term).

Double-bar. The double line drawn at the end of a piece, or at the end of one of its definite sections. The double-bar which generally occurs about a third of the way through a sonata-form movement (after the exposition) is an important point of momentary rest, from which a new beginning is made.

CONCERT-GOER'S GLOSSARY 87

Double-Bass. See pp. 59, 60.
Double Bassoon or **Contrafagotto.** See p. 61.
Double Counterpoint. (See **Counterpoint,** p. 6) Double counterpoint is counterpoint in two voices which may be 'inverted' (the lower voice becoming the higher) and still sound good.
Drammatico (It.). Dramatic; *Drammaticamente*, dramatically.
Drone Bass. A persistent note in the bass, producing a bagpipe (q.v.) effect.
Drum. See pp. 62, 63, and also **Side Drum** and **Chromatic Drum.**
Dulcimer. An instrument consisting of stretched wires played by hammers held in the hands. A piano is nothing but a perfected dulcimer.
Duple Time. Time with two beats in a bar. See **Bar.**

Écossaise (Fr.). A piece in the style of a lively Scottish dance.
Elegy. An instrumental composition of a mournful character.
Energico (It.). Energetic.
English Horn = **Cor Anglais.** See p. 61.
Enharmonic. Having intervals less than a semitone, e.g. the interval from C sharp to D flat. On a keyboard instrument, therefore, no enharmonic intervals are (strictly) possible. Enharmonic modulation is a change of key brought about by, for instance, using a chord with a C sharp and then considering this a D flat, and so shifting into a key of which this latter note forms a part.
Enunciation = *Exposition* in sonata form. See Ch. VI and subsequent chapters.
Episode in Fugue. See p. 44.
Equali (It.). Pieces for instruments of the same kind, e.g. Beethoven's *Equali* for Trombones.
Eroica (It.). Heroic For Symphony with this title see **Beethoven.**

DLGD

Espressivo (It.). In an expressive manner.
Esquisse (Fr.). A sketch—a fancy title for a short picturesque piece of instrumental music.
Étude (Fr.) = Study (q.v.).
Euphonium. See **Saxhorn.**
Exposition. (*a*) The first part of a sonata-form movement, in which the subjects are 'exposed' (also called *Enunciation*). (Ch. VI.) (*b*) The first part of a fugue, in which the subject appears in all the voices. (see Ch. VIII.)
Expression. Music as human expression. See Ch. III and p. 21.

f, ff. See **Forte.**
Fagotto (It.). The Bassoon. See p. 61.
False Close. See **Cadence.**
Fandango. A dance form in three or six-beat time. It is of Spanish origin, and implies the use of castanets (q.v.).
Fanfare. A trumpet flourish.
Fantasia (It.). A piece in free style. The term *Free Fantasia* is sometimes used as a description of the development (see Ch. VI) in sonata form.
Feroce (It.). Fierce.
Figured Bass. A bass part with figures under or above it, indicating the chords to be played. From this vague indication, in the Purcell-Bach-Handel days, the player of the harpsichord in the orchestra, or of the organ in church, would work out his part as he played Nowadays figured bass remains only as an exercise for harmony students, and even as that is rapidly disappearing.
Finale (It.). The ending of a piece, or the end 'movement' in a sonata or similar work.
Fioriture (It.). Flourishes, embellishments.
Flat. See pp. 3, 4.
Flute. See pp. 60, 61.
Folk Music. Music composed by the musically illiterate peasantry,

as, for instance, many songs and dance tunes.
Form. See p. 6, and Chs. II to X.
Forte (It.) or **f**, loud; **ff** = **fortissimo** (It.), very loud.
Forza (It.). Force, e.g. *Con tutta forza*, with all possible power.
Fugato (It.). See p. 47.
Fughetta (It.). A small fugue.
Fugue. See Ch. VIII; in oratorio and in Overture, p. 55.
Full Close. See **Cadence**.
Fuoco (It.). Fire, e.g. *Con fuoco*, with fire, dash, 'go'.
Furioso (It.). Furiously.

Gajo or **Gaio** (It.). Gay.
Galliard. A fairly lively old dance form in three-beat time, common in the suites of the Elizabethan composers.
Gavotte. A dance form in four-beat time.
Gigue = Jig. A lively dance form in three, six, nine, or twelve-beat time, which formed one of the movements of the old suites.
Giocoso (It.). Jocose.
Gitano (It.). In the style of gipsy music.
Giubilo (It.). Joy.
Giubiloso (It.). In a jubilant manner.
Giusto (It.). Exact, e.g. *Tempo giusto*, strict time.
Glissando (It.). (*a*) A gliding from note to note on bowed instruments, i.e. a sliding down or up the banister instead of going down or up the stairs, so to speak. (*b*) A rapid playing of a scale passage on the piano by drawing the thumb or finger along the keys.
Glockenspiel (Ger.). See p. 63.
Gong. Needs no description. Occasionally used orchestrally.
Grandezza (It.). Dignity.
Grave (It.). Solemn.
Gravità (It.). Gravity.
Graziosamente (It.). Gracefully.
Grazioso (It.). Graceful.
Ground Bass (or *Basso ostinato*). A recurring bass part with the upper parts varied on each recurrence, thus a sort of variations form. Purcell and Bach used this form very finely. See **Chaconne** and **Passacaglia**.
Gruppo, Gruppetto (It.). A certain little melodic figure, otherwise called a turn (q.v.).
Guerriero (It.). Warlike.
Guitar. A six-stringed, plucked instrument.

Half-Cadence or **Half-Close**. See **Cadence**.
Harmonics in string playing. See p. 60.
Harmony. See pp. 6, 8.
Harp. See p. 63.
Harpsichord. A keyboard instrument. The precursor of the pianoforte, from which it differed chiefly in that its strings were plucked by quills instead of struck by hammers. It has recently been revived, and is now quite often heard.
Hautbois (Fr.) or **Hautboy** = Oboe. See pp. 58, 61.
Heckelphone. A sort of baritone oboe, invented by one Heckel, and comparatively lately brought into a little use by Strauss.
Horn. See p. 62.

Idée Fixe (Fr.). See p. 53.
Idyl, Idyll. A poetic piece of romantic character.
Imitation. The taking up by one voice or part of some little bit of melody just performed by another.
Imperfect Cadence. See **Cadence**.
Impromptu. A quasi-extempory short piece of instrumental music.
Incidental Music. Music occurring in a play, or intended to be performed between the acts, &c.
In modo di (It.). In the style of, e.g. *In modo di Marcia Funèbre*, in the style of a funeral march.
Interlude. A piece intended to be played *between*, e.g. between the acts of a play.
Intermezzo. Originally an instrumental piece interpolated (e.g.

in an opera); now often a short instrumental piece for independent performance.

Interrupted Cadence. See **Cadence.**

Interval. The difference in pitch between one note and another. Intervals are called by number names, as, for instance, a fifth (= an interval of which the two notes are five notes apart in the scale—inclusive.)

Introduction. The opening passage sometimes prefixed to a sonata, symphony, or other work. See pp. 26, 30, 40.

Invention. Bach wrote keyboard pieces so styled, highly contrapuntal in form. They are much used as studies in part-playing by pianists.

Inversion. The turning upside-down (*a*) of an interval or chord, i.e. the putting of one of the original lower notes into the treble; (*b*) of a melody, the changing it so that all its ascending notes descend and *vice versa* (this is a mere rough-and-ready definition, but sufficient for the present purpose); (*c*) of counterpoint, the putting of an upper melody lower and a lower melody higher, so that they change places. (See **Double Counterpoint.**)

Invertible Counterpoint. See **Double Counterpoint.**

Irato (It.). Angry.

Kapellmeister = *Capellmeister* (q.v.).

Kettledrums. See pp. 62, 63.

Key. See pp. 1–4, 23.

Konzertstück = *Concertstück* (q.v.).

Lamentoso (It.). In the manner of a lament.

Ländler (Ger.). A sort of slow waltz.

Langsam (Ger.). Slow.

Languido (It.). Weak, languid.

Larghetto (It.). Rather slow and stately (diminutive of *Largo*).

Largo (It.). Slow and stately.

Leading motif or **Leitmotif** (Ger.) or **Leitmotiv** (Ger.). See pp. 53, 56.

Leading Note. The seventh note of the key, so called because it has a feeling of upward tendency to the key-note or tonic.

Legato (It.). Lit. 'bound together', i.e. the notes smoothly joined to one another; the opposite of *Staccato*.

Leggieramente (It.). Lightly.

Leggiero (It.). Light.

Legno (It.). See **Col legno.**

Leitmotif or **Leitmotiv** (Ger.). Leading *Motif*, pp. 53, 56.

Lentamente (It.). Slowly.

Lento (It.) or **Lent** (Fr.). Slow.

Lesson. A suite (q.v.) for harpsichord or other instrument, in Handel's time.

Libretto (It.). The word-book of an opera or oratorio.

Licenza (It.). Licence, freedom.

Lied (plural **Lieder**) (Ger.). A song, or instrumental piece in song style (*Lieder ohne Worte* = Songs without words. See p. 22).

Loure. (*a*) A bagpipe. (*b*) A dance form with a bagpipe effect.

Louré (Fr.). Legato (q.v.). Strictly, in the style of a loure, but used in violin music to indicate that each note is to be articulated but the passage played with one bow. The sign is a little dash over each note.

Lugubre (Fr.). Dreary, lugubrious in style.

Lute. An instrument of the guitar kind popular in Elizabethan days.

Madrigal. See p. 69.

Maestoso (It.). Majestic.

Major Scale. See pp. 2, 3.

Malinconico (It.). Melancholy.

Manuals. The hand keyboards of the organ (of which there may be one, two, three, four, or five), as distinguished from the foot keyboard, i.e. the Pedals. See **Organ.**

Marcato (It.). Marked, i.e. heavily accented.

March. The name explains itself.

An analysis of a march will be found on p. 26. Pieces in this style are occasionally used as sonata or symphony movements. See pp. 37, 38.

Marcia (It.). March.

Marziale (It.). In a martial style, or in a March style.

Mass. A musical setting of the Communion Service of the Roman or Lutheran Church. (Sixteenth-century Masses, see p. 69.)

Mazurka. A dance form of Polish origin in three-beat time. Chopin wrote mazurkas for piano.

Measure. See **Bar**. *Measure* is invariably used in America and to some extent in Britain for *Bar* in the sense of the portion of music between two bar lines. It is to be wished that this usage might be generally adopted.

Mediant. The third note of the key.

Meno (It.). Less.

Menuetto. Minuet (q.v.).

Minim. One of the longer notes in music; equal to half a semibreve or two crotchets.

Minor Scale. See pp. 2, 3.

Minuet. A piece in three-beat time and in the style of the dance of that name. It often appeared as one of the movements of the sonata and symphony, being later a good deal superseded by the Scherzo. See pp. 22, 37.

Misterioso (It.). Mysterious.

Misurato (It.). Lit. 'measured', i.e. in strict time.

Moderato (It.). At a moderate speed.

Modes. The old scales, which began to go out of general use by composers in the early seventeenth century (see p. 69), but which are still drawn upon for special purposes. Sometimes they are called the Church Modes.

Modulation. See pp. 4, 30.

Molto (It.). Much, very, e.g. *Molto adagio*, very slow.

Mordent or **Mordente.** A particular little ornamental treatment of a note, in which it is alternated with the note above or below.

Morendo (It.). Dying away.

Mosso (It.). Moved; hence *Più mosso*, more quickly; *Meno mosso*, less quickly, &c.

Motet. An anthem in the Catholic or Lutheran Church, generally unaccompanied.

Motif. See pp. 30, 56, 75.

Moto (It.). Motion; hence *Con moto*, quickly; *Moto perpetuo*, 'perpetual motion' (applied to a piece with continuous quick notes).

Motto Theme. In programme music (q.v.) a theme to which some more or less fanciful symbolic significance is applied, and which carries this with it through the composition. Cf. Wagner's *Motifs* (pp. 56, 75).

Movement. See p. 35.

Musette. (*a*) An instrument of the bagpipe (q.v.) type. (*b*) A kind of oboe. (*c*) A sort of gavotte with a drone-bass suggesting the bagpipes.

Music-Drama. See pp. 56, 75.

Mute. (*a*) In stringed instruments, see p. 67. (*b*) In wind instruments (as, for instance, horns and trumpets) the mute is generally a sort of pad placed in the bell of the instrument to soften the tone or change it in quality.

Nachtmusik (Ger.). A nightpiece. (See **Nocturne** and **Notturno**.)

Natural. A note unchanged by the addition of any sharp or flat. (See p. 3.) A sign used to contradict a sharp or flat previously used.

Nobilmente (It.). In a noble manner.

Nocturne (Fr.). Properly a nightpiece. A short instrumental piece of a romantic character, generally for piano, with a melody in the right hand and accompaniment in the left. The Irishman, John Field, invented nocturnes, and Chopin followed him. (Cf. **Nachtmusik** and **Notturno**.) See pp. 22, 25.

Nonet. A piece for nine voices or instruments.

Notturno (It.). A Night-piece. Cf. **Nocturne** and **Nachtmusik**.)

Obbligato or **Obligato** (It.). Properly a part which must be played; latterly, however, a part which can be dispensed with, as for instance, a *Violin Obbligato* to a song, which is additional to the piano accompaniment and, though desirable of performance, not essential.

Oboe. See pp. 58, 61.

Oboe da Caccia. An obsolete form of the cor anglais. (See p. 61.)

Oboe d'Amore. A sort of mezzo-soprano oboe, obsolete until revived by Strauss.

Octet. A piece for eight voices or instruments.

Ode. A musical setting of a single poem on a more or less extended scale.

Offertoire (Fr.) or **Offertorium** (Ger.). Music played or sung (*a*) during the offering of the elements, or (*b*) during the collection in a Church service.

Open String. In bowed instruments a string which is being played without the finger being pressed on it, and thus giving its own prime note.

Opéra Comique does not mean comic opera, but opera including spoken dialogue.

Ophicleide. A bass brass instrument, now rare, but written for in some scores by composers of a few generations back, e.g. Berlioz and Mendelssohn.

Opus (or **Op.**). See p. 7.

Oratorio. A sacred work for solo vocalists, chorus, and orchestra, other than a setting of any part of the church service. See Ch. X and p. 72.

Orchestration. The same as Scoring (q.v.). See also pp. 72, 74, and Chs. XI and XII.

Ordinario (It.) = Ordinary, e.g. *Tempo ordinario*, at an ordinary rate of speed.

Organ. Just as the piano is the dulcimer (q.v.) perfected, so is the organ the panpipes multiplied and mechanicalized. There are a large number of 'stops', each consisting of one set of such panpipes, and some of these are allotted to the one, two, three, four, or five *Manual* keyboards, and others to the *Pedal* keyboard. The various sets of panpipes can be brought into action by the pulling of the appropriate stop knobs (themselves often called 'stops'). Some of the stops are made up of plain pipes called the 'flue pipes', and others of pipes with reeds (cf. p. 61) called 'reed pipes'. The basis of good organ tone is in the plain diapason stops. Some stops are intended to be imitative of orchestral instruments, as *Flute, Clarinet, Oboe, Trumpet*, &c. The chief manual of the organ is called the *Great Organ*; the others are called *Swell Organ, Choir Organ, Solo Organ*, and (sometimes) *Echo Organ*. The organ is comparatively rarely used with the orchestra.

Ostinato (It.). Obstinate, hence continual or frequently repeated. *Basso ostinato* = *Ground Bass* (q.v.).

Overture. See p. 55. Overtures for performance as independent pieces are now often composed—'Concert Overtures'.

Ovvero (It.). Or, e.g. *Adagio ovvero largo*.

p, pp. See **Piano**.

Part. The music for any one particular voice or instrument of a combination. See p. 42.

Partita (It.). *Suite* (q.v.).

Passacaglia (It.). Much the same as *Chaconne* (q.v.).
Passepied (Fr.) or **Paspy**. A bright three-beat dance.
Passion Music. Settings in oratorio style of the story of the Passion, by Bach and others.
Pastourelle (Fr.). (*a*) A pastoral piece. (*b*) One of the movements of a quadrille.
Pavane (Fr.). A rather solemn dance form.
Pedal (of Organ). The foot-keyboard as distinguished from the Manuals (q.v.). (See **Organ**.)
Pedal in Fugue. See p. 46.
Pedal Clarinet. See **Contrabass Clarinet**.
Pentatonic Scale. See **Scale**.
Percussion Instruments. See p. 62.
Perfect Cadence. See **Cadence**.
Perfect 4th. The interval of a 4th containing five semitones, e.g. the 4th which lies between the tonic and the subdominant.
Perfect 5th. The interval of a 5th containing seven semitones, e.g. the 5th which lies between the tonic and dominant.
Pesante (It.). Heavy.
Pezzo (It.). A piece.
Phantasy. A title given to pieces by early composers, e.g. the Elizabethan English composers. The term was, in the early twentieth century, applied by the late W. W. Cobbett (Maecenas of British chamber music) to pieces for string trio, quartet, &c. in one movement—a form developed by the younger British composers at his instigation.
Phrase. See p. 5.
Piacevole (It.). Pleasant, graceful.
Piano (It.) or **p.** soft. **pp** = **pianissimo**, very soft.
Pianoforte (It.). Lit. soft-loud. So called to distinguish it from its precursor, the harpsichord (q.v.) which had not the same power of varying its tone. For development of piano music see Ch. XIII.

Pianoforte Concerto. A concerto (see p. 35) in which the piano takes the solo part.
Pibroch. A sort of Scottish bagpipe music, generally variations on an air—sometimes in the nature of a lament, sometimes warlike in character.
Piccolo. See pp. 60, 61.
Pièce Lyrique (Fr.). A lyrical piece, a short piece in more or less of a song style.
Più. More, e.g. *Più forte*, more loudly.
Pizzicato (It.). Plucked (used of instruments normally bowed). See p. 60.
Plagal Cadence. See **Cadence**.
Pochetto or **Pochettino** (It.). A very little (diminutive of *Poco*).
Poco (It.). A little (e.g. *Poco lento*, rather slow); *Poco a poco*, little by little, by degrees.
Polacca = *Polonaise* (q.v.).
Polonaise (*Polacca*). A piece written in the style of a particular Polish dance. Chopin is the most famous composer of the polonaise, expressing his sense of nationality therein.
Polyphony. 'Many-voicedness', or Counterpoint. See p. 6.
Pomposo (It.). Pompous.
Potpourri (Fr.). A medley of tunes.
Praeludium, A prelude, or piece which might be used as a prelude to play; the first piece of a suite or the opening piece of a concert, &c.
Pregando (It.). Prayerfully.
Preghiera (It.). A prayer.
Prelude. Properly piece intended to precede another, e.g. *Prelude and Fugue*. See p. 53.
Presque (Fr.). Almost.
Presto (It.). Rapid.
Primo (It.). First, e.g. *Tempo primo* = at the same speed as at the beginning of the piece.
Programme Music. See Ch. IX.
Prologue. A vocal solo introductory to an opera, &c.
Pulse = Beat. See p. 4.

CONCERT-GOER'S GLOSSARY

Quadruple Time. Time with four beats in a bar. (See **Bar**.)

Quarter-Tone. Half a semitone. Such an interval can, of course, be played on a bowed, but not on a keyed, instrument.

Quartet. A piece for four voices or instruments. If for four stringed instruments, it is called a *String Quartet*; if for three stringed instruments and one other instrument it is called by the name of the latter, e.g. *Piano Quartet*.

Quasi (It.). Almost, as if.

Quatuor (Fr.) = *Quartet* (q.v.).

Quaver. One of the shorter notes in music, of the value of half a crotchet.

Quintet. A piece for five voices or instruments. If for four stringed instruments and one other it is called by the name of the latter, e.g. *Clarinet Quintet, Piano Quintet*.

Rallentando (It.). Getting gradually slower.

Recapitulation. See pp. 31–33.

Recitative. See pp. 55, 70, 73.

Reed Instruments. See p. 61.

Register. All voices and instruments differ in quality of tone in the different portions of their range. These different portions are called *Registers*.

Related Key. See p. 4.

Requiem. A Mass for the dead.

Resolution. See **Dissonance**.

Rest. A sign in musical notation denoting silence.

Rhapsody. An instrumental piece generally of a rather ecstatic character.

Rhythm. See pp. 4, 23.

Ripieno (It.). Lit. a filling-up. In earlier eighteenth-century music players who only came in in the full passages were so described in contradistinction to *Concertino* (q.v.).

Risoluto (It.). Resolute in style.

Ritardando (It.). Getting gradually slower.

Ritornel or **Ritornello** (It.). (*a*) A bit of instrumental music prefixed or affixed to, or interpolated in a song. (*b*) Something repeated, as for instance a theme given out in a concerto by the solo instrument and then taken up by the full orchestra.

Romance. In English this means an instrumental piece of simple song-like character; in French, a song.

Romantic. A term of doubtful and varying significance, explained on pp. 74–75.

Romanza (It.) = Romance. A short instrumental piece of song-like character.

Rondo. See pp. 23, 33, 36.

Rondo-Sonata Form. See p. 39.

Rosalia. A *Sequence* (q.v.), rising a note at each repetition.

Rubato (It.). Lit. 'robbed'. *Tempo rubato* = 'robbed time', i.e. having certain notes slightly shortened in playing, at the player's discretion, in order to lengthen others. It may also denote the acceleration of quite a lengthy passage, balanced by a corresponding retardation, for expressive purposes.

Salterello (It.) or **Saltarelle** (Fr.). A light type of dance in three-beat or six-beat time.

Sarabande. A piece in slow three-beat dance rhythm, which found a place in the seventeenth and eighteenth-century suites.

Sarrusophone. See **Oboe** and **Clarinet** (p. 61). A brass instrument with an oboe mouthpiece (i.e. double reed). The contrabass sarrusophone is sometimes used instead of the double bassoon.

Saxhorns. Brass instruments on the cornet model, invented by one Sax. They are much used in military and brass bands. The three bass saxhorns call for most attention here, as they are in varying measure used in Orchestras. They are: (*a*) *Bass Saxhorn in B flat* or *Euphonium;* (*b*) *Bass Saxhorn in E flat* or *Bombardon* or *Contrabass Tuba;* and (*c*) *Contrabass Saxhorn in B flat*, also called *Bombardon* or *Contrabass Tuba*.

The indication 'Tuba' in an orchestral score generally refers to (*b*), i.e. the *Bass Saxhorn in E flat* or to the same instrument a tone higher, i.e. in F. It may be recognized from the fact that it looks like a giant cornet, inverted in performance, and with a mouthpiece brought over to the side. There is, unfortunately, as will be seen above, some confusion in the names of these instruments, and other names are sometimes used which do not tally with those given above.

Saxophone. A brass instrument with a clarinet mouthpiece and reed used in French military bands and in dance bands, and occasionally written for in orchestral scores by French and other composers. The saxophone ranks with the woodwind, not the brass. Cf. **Sarrusophone**.

Scale. See pp. 1–3. *Diatonic Scales* are the ordinary major and minor scales. *Chromatic Scales* are scales proceeding entirely by Semitones. The *Whole-tone Scale* is a scale made up entirely of tones (try it on the piano and get its effect into the ear; Debussy has popularized it). The *Pentatonic Scale* is the scale of five notes used by the Chinese, the Bantu, and other races; some Scottish tunes also are in this scale. For development of the diatonic scales see pp. 69, 72.

Scena (It.). A solo vocal piece of large scope and dramatic style, generally in an opera.

Scherzo (It.). Properly a *joke*, hence a jocular instrumental piece, as some of Beethoven's symphony and sonata middle movements. Often, however, merely a *lively* piece. In the more modern sonatas and symphonies the Scherzo takes the place of the old Minuet. See p. 37.

Scoring = Orchestration. Generally the writing out in orchestral score of a piece previously composed, so far as its form and content are concerned.

Sehr (Ger.). Very.

Semibreve. One of the longest notes used in music the equal in value of half a breve, or two minims.

Semiquaver. One of the shorter notes used in music, the equal in value of half a quaver.

Semitone. See p. 2, also **Chromatic Semitone** and **Diatonic Semitone**.

Semplice (It.). In a simple style.

Sempre (It.). Always, continually, e.g. *Sempre forte*, loud all the time.

Sentence. See p. 5.

Senza (It.). Without, e.g. *Senza sordini*. See **Sordino**.

Septet. A piece for seven voices or instruments.

Septuor (Fr.) = *Septet* (q.v.).

Sequence. The immediate repetition of a passage at a higher or lower pitch. The use of rising sequences is one way of increasing excitement, and the use of descending sequences a way of calming down the feelings of an audience. See **Rosalia**.

Sérénade (Fr.) (= *Abendmusik*, Ger.). An 'evening piece', such as could be played beneath the windows of one's lady-love. Cf. **Aubade**.

Serpent. An obsolete wooden bass wind instrument.

Sestetto (It.) = *Sextet* (q.v.).

Settimetto (It.) = *Septet* (q.v.)

Sextet. A piece for six voices or instruments.

Sextolet or **Sextuplet.** A group of six notes to a beat or of six notes in the usual time of four.

sf = **Sforzando** or **Sforzato** (It.).

'Forced', i.e. strongly accented; applied to an individual note or chord.

Shake. An embellishment consisting of rapid alternation of a note with the note above.

Sharp. See pp. 3–4.

Siciliano (It.). An old dance form in six-beat or twelve-beat time.

Side Drum, or **Snare Drum.** A drum the lower end of which has 'snares' or pieces of catgut stretched tightly across so as to rattle when the upper end is struck.

Signature. For *Time-Signature*, see p. 5. *Key-Signature* means the sharps or flats placed at the beginning of each stave or line of a piece of music, showing its key. See **Key,** pp. 1–3.

Sinfonia (It.). A symphony.

Snare Drum. See **Side Drum.**

Sonata Form. See Chs. VI and VII.

Song Cycle. A series of songs, connected in thought and intended to be performed as a set.

Songs without words. See pp. 22, 36.

Sonoramente (It.). Sonorously.

Soprano. See **Treble.**

Sordamente. Subdued.

Sordino (It.). Mute, or damper. Hence: (*a*) In the case of bowed instruments, *Con Sordini* = with mutes; *Senza Sordini* = without mutes (see p. 60). (*b*) In the case of piano, *Senza Sordini* = without the dampers, i.e. use the right pedal; *Con Sordini* = with dampers, i.e. cease using the pedal.

Sostenuto (It.). Sustained in style.

Sotto voce (It.). In a mere whisper.

Spiccato (It.). Detached in style. applied to bowed instrument playing in which the bow is used in a springing way to produce this effect.

Staccato (It.). Detached. Applied to notes which the performer must sustain for less than their normal value. A dot or dash over a note also indicates this.

Strepitoso (It.). Boisterously.

Stretto in Fugue. See p. 46.

Stringendo (It.). Lit. 'drawing together', i.e. getting quicker and quicker.

Strings. See p. 59.

Study (or **Étude**). A short piece developing some particular point in technique as an exercise for the player. Sometimes the study is written at great length and in brilliant style for concert performance, and is called Concert Study, or Symphonic Study. Études, however, are not always merely technically difficult; they may be quite poetic, e.g. Chopin's Études.

Subdominant. The note immediately below the *Dominant*, i.e. the fourth note of the key.

Subject. Of sonata or symphony, see Ch. VI and subsequent chapters. of a fugue, see Ch. VIII.

Submediant. The sixth note of the key.

Suite. A set of short pieces of varied and contrasting character meant to be performed as one long piece. Originally (sixteenth and seventeenth centuries) the short pieces were largely modelled on various national dances. The Elizabethan composers, and Purcell, Bach, and Handel, wrote much of their instrumental music in this form. The sonata and symphony have grown out of the suite, but the latter still persists and is frequently used by composers. The minuet in many sonatas and symphonies is a dance relic of the original suites.

Supertonic. The note next above the tonic in the scale (i.e. the second note of the key).

Suspension. A note held on from a previous chord and left sounding with the next chord, of which it does not form a real part, then dropping to the note below, which does form such a part.

Symphonic Poem. See pp. 53, 54.

Symphonic Variations. Variations (see p. 26) on a large scale, amounting in importance to a movement of the symphony type.

Symphony. See p. 35 and whole of Chs. VI and VII.

Syncopation. Displacement of the accent, as, for instance, is done in jazz.

Tambour de basque. (Fr.) = Tambourine.

Tambourine. Unnecessary to describe this. Used occasionally in the orchestra, especially to give Spanish colouring. See p. 63.

Tanto (It.). So much, too much, e.g. *Lento ma non tanto*—'go slow but don't overdo it'.

Tarantella (It.). A lively Italian dance in six-beat time, supposed to be a cure for the bite of the tarantula spider, hence its name.

Tema con variazioni (It.). Theme (= air) with variations. See p. 26.

Tempestuoso (It.). In a tempestuous manner.

Tempo (It.). Speed.

Teneramente (It.). Tenderly.

Tenero (It.). Tender.

Tenor. (*a*) The third voice down in an ordinary mixed voice choir or male voice church choir. So called because it used to *hold* the chief part, or melody, in hymn-tunes, &c. (which is now usually given to the trebles). (*b*) The viola (also called 'Alto'). See p. 59.

Ternary Form. See pp. 24, 55.

Time. See p. 4.

Time-Signature. See p. 4.

Timpani (It.). Kettledrums. See pp. 62–63.

Toccata (It.). A brilliant piece of rapid movement.

Tonality. The sense of Key. See pp. 1–3.

Tone. See p. 2.

Tone Colour. Quality of tone, e.g. 'the oboe has a tone-colour different from that of the clarinet'. (See pp. 58, 61.) The term is sometimes used of piano playing, as a good player at a fine instrument can produce many different qualities of tone.

Tone Painting. The sort of thing described in the chapter on *Programme Music* (Ch. IX).

Tone Poem. See p. 53.

Tonic. The key-note.

Tornando (It.). Returning.

Tranquillo (It.). Tranquil.

Transcription. (*a*) The re-arranging of a piece for another instrument or combination of instruments than that for which it was originally composed. The same thing as **Arrangement**. (*b*) The making of a potpourri of melodies from an opera, &c., for some instrument.

Transformation of Themes. See p. 53.

Treble. (*a*) The highest part of the harmony; (*b*) the highest voice of the normal choir; (*c*) the highest instrument of the combination. As the highest voice in the choir the word has an alternative, *Soprano*.

Tremolo, Tremulo, a form of *Vibrato* (q.v.). *Tremolando* = with a Tremolo.

Très (Fr.). Very, e.g. *Très vite*, very fast.

Triangle. A metal percussion instrument of no defined pitch. See p. 63.

Trill. *See* **Shake**.

Trio. (*a*) A piece for three voices or instruments. If for three stringed instruments it is called a *String Trio*. If for two stringed instruments and one other instrument it is called by the name of the latter, e.g. *Piano Trio*. (*b*) A section used in the Minuet-Trio-Minuet movement of a symphony or sonata (see p. 37), or a piece similarly used with a scherzo (scherzo-Trio-Scherzo), or a section of a march, similarly used.

Triple Counterpoint. See **Counterpoint** (p. 6) and **Double Counterpoint** in this Glossary. Triple counterpoint is a combination of three melodies which

may be rearranged in any order and still sound well.
Triple Time. A time with three beats in a bar. See **Bar**.
Triplet. Three notes played in the time of two.
Trombone. See p. 62.
Troppo (It.). Too much, generally used with negative, *Non troppo*, e.g. *Allegro ma non troppo* = Quick, but not too much so.
Trumpet. See p. 62.
Tuba. See p. 62; also under **Saxhorn**.
Tubular Bells. See p. 63.
Turn. A little embellishment of a note consisting in old music of the note above, the note itself, the note below, and then the principal note again (four notes in all). In music of more recent date the turn generally begins with the principal note (five notes in all).
Tutti (It.). All. Indicates the entrance of the whole chorus or instrumental force. The special use of the word is in concertos, where after the solo instrument has had its innings the full band comes in. The word is often used as a noun, indicating a passage of the kind mentioned.
Tympani (incorrect spelling of 'Timpani'). See p. 62.

Valse (Fr.) (= Waltz, Ger.). A dance form in three-beat time.

Variations. See pp. 26, 37, 38, 53.
Veloce (It.). Rapid.
Velocissimo (It.). Very rapid.
Vibrato (It.). A trembling effect in singing or in the playing of bowed instruments. See **Tremolo**.
Vif (Fr.). Lively.
Viola. See pp. 59, 60.
Viola da Gamba. One of the old viol family which preceded the violins. As its name implies, the viola da gamba was held between the legs, like a modern violoncello.
Violin. See pp. 59, 60.
Violin Concerto. A concerto (q.v.) in which the violin takes the principal part.
Violoncello. See pp. 59, 60.
Virtuoso (It.). An accomplished performer.
Vivace (It.). Lively.
Vivacissimo (It.). Very lively.
Vivo (It.). Brisk, full of life.
'Voices' in a fugue. See p. 42.

Waltz = **Valse.** A dance form in three-beat time. For analysis of a waltz by Chopin, see p. 24.
Whole-tone Scale. See **Scale**.
Wood-wind. See p. 60.

Xylophone. An instrument with pieces of wood of varying lengths struck by hammers held in the hands.

ADDENDA

Aleatory. The composer requires random improvisation within specified limits (from Latin *aleae*, dice).

Electronic Music. An ordered arrangement of sounds generated by oscillators, modified in various ways, and then recorded.

Musique Concrète (Fr.). A 'picture' built up of natural sounds which are recorded and then modified, e.g. reversed, played at different speeds, mixed together.

Serial Composition. Music based on a series of notes, usually twelve (Note-Row), which can be inverted or reversed.

Twelve-Note Music. See **Serial Composition**.